D1617434

FREEDOM AND
REASON

FREEDOM AND REASON

BY

R. M. HARE

FELLOW OF BALLIOL COLLEGE
OXFORD

OXFORD
AT THE CLARENDON PRESS

Oxford University Press, Amen House, London E.C.4

GLASGOW NEW YORK TORONTO MELBOURNE WELLINGTON
BOMBAY CALCUTTA MADRAS KARACHI LAHORE DACCA
CAPE TOWN SALISBURY NAIROBI IBADAN ACCRA
KUALA LUMPUR HONG KONG

FIRST PUBLISHED 1963
REPRINTED LITHOGRAPHICALLY AT THE
UNIVERSITY PRESS, OXFORD
FROM CORRECTED SHEETS OF THE FIRST EDITION
1964

PRINTED IN GREAT BRITAIN

PREFACE

THE function of moral philosophy—or at any rate the hope with which I study it—is that of helping us to think better about moral questions by exposing the logical structure of the language in which this thought is expressed. When I wrote my first book, which was a study of the chief moral words, I had no more than a dim notion of what account of moral reasoning would develop out of this study—only the conviction that, if it were well done, our understanding of moral questions would be increased. In the years since, this hope has not proved entirely vain; and, although I am still far from clear on many matters, I think it worth while to publish this progress report, if only to enlist the help of others in becoming clearer.

My views have been the subject of a great deal of controversy; but any reader who is looking in this book for a full-scale rebuttal of my critics will be disappointed. I did, indeed, in preparation for writing it, draft about fifty pages of polemical matter in answer to the most widely canvassed objections; but, having thus convinced myself that they could be answered, I came to feel that the answers to them were less exciting than the positive things which I had to say, and possibly of less durable interest; I therefore put them aside, to appear elsewhere. I have profited greatly from these discussions; but I am obstinate enough to believe that, though they have added much to what I thought before, they have not taken much away.

There will be found, therefore, in this book, only passing allusions to these wrangles. Lest they should be thought to be directed at the views of particular people, I must make clear that, in all cases except where names are mentioned, the views referred to are ones which I have heard in discussion, but cannot ascribe to any identifiable person. I must, however, express my thanks to a great many identifiable, but for reasons of space unidentified, people, for the interest which they have shown in my opinions, and for the help they have given me in finding out what objections I have to meet.

Much has been omitted besides polemics, for the same reasons as were given in the preface to my first book. In particular, I have, as before, left two or three palpable loose ends, knowing that any book about moral reasoning is bound to be incomplete wherever it stops. For example, I have devoted only a very short digression to the problem of free will; a whole book would be required to say anything useful about this problem. I have, on similar grounds, contented myself with pointing out certain affinities between my own position and that of the writers of the utilitarian tradition; I have left unanswered many questions which must be asked by anybody who wishes to produce a watertight theory of this sort. Here, as in many other places, I have tried only to provide material for future discussion.

Books and articles are constantly appearing on the subject of moral language and moral thought; and if I may seem to have ignored most of them, I have the excuse that to have attempted to read them all would have put an end to my hopes of writing anything. Those which I have read were picked out more by chance than by any considered policy or assessment of the merits of their authors; I have learnt much from them, and can only ask the forgiveness of those whose work I have neglected. These, I am sure, include many who have criticized me; perhaps they may find, in the positive views here put forward, some defence against their criticisms.

I owe a great debt of thanks to the Council of Humanities of Princeton University for appointing me, in the autumn of 1957, to the fellowship which gave the opportunity to start

writing this book under ideal conditions; to my colleagues in
the department there for much stimulating discussion; and
to my own college, Balliol, for setting me free for that term.

It is written for all who are seriously troubled by moral
questions, and dedicated especially to my children. May it be
that, through the discussion of the problems of ethics, the
world in which they have to live may be one in which these
matters are better understood.

R. M. H.

Balliol College
1962

CONTENTS

PART I

DESCRIBING AND PRESCRIBING

> He to whom thou was sent for ease, being by name *Legality*,
> is the son of the Bond-woman . . . how canst thou expect
> by them to be made free?
>
> BUNYAN, The Pilgrim's Progress

1 · INTRODUCTION

1.1. I ASK the reader to start by supposing that someone (himself perhaps) is faced with a serious moral problem—one that calls forth all the powers of thought, imagination, and feeling that a man possesses. He will have to supply his own example; for I cannot say for any one of my readers what moral question has troubled him most. If he cannot think of an example, he will not understand this book, and may as well postpone the reading of it until he has lived a little longer.

I wish to draw attention to two features which any such serious moral problem will have, the combination of which seems to confront us, as philosophers, with a paradox, or even an antinomy. The first is that a man who is faced with such a problem knows that it is his own problem, and that nobody can answer it for him. He may, it is true, ask the advice of other people; and he may also ascertain more facts about the circumstances and consequences of a proposed action, and other facts of this sort. But there will come a time when he does not hope to find out anything else of relevance by factual inquiry, and when he knows that, whatever others may say about the answer to his problem, *he* has to answer it. If anyone were to suggest that the answer must be such and such, because everybody says so—or that, even, he would be abusing the English language if he gave any other answer—he will, if he understands what moral questions are, feel that to accept these suggestions would be to accept a diminution of his own freedom. For one of the most important constituents of our freedom, as moral agents, is the freedom to form our own opinions about moral questions, even if that involves changing our language.

It might be objected that moral questions are not peculiar in this respect—that we are free also to form our own opinions about such matters as whether the world is round. In a sense this is true; but we are free to form our own moral opinions in a much stronger sense than this. For if we say that the world is flat, we can in principle be shown certain facts such that, once we have admitted them, we cannot go on saying that the world is flat without being guilty either of self-contradiction or of a misuse of language. That nothing of this sort can be done in morals is a thesis which must have the support of all those who reject naturalism. I shall not now argue this thesis, since I have done so before; I shall later, in passing, bring forward certain further arguments against naturalism, and against attempts to revive it in more sophisticated forms. But for the moment let us assume that there can be no logical deduction of moral judgements from statements of fact. If this be once granted, it follows that we are free to form our own moral opinions in a much stronger sense than we are free to form our own opinions as to what the facts are.

1.2. Against this conviction, which every adult has, that he is free to form his own opinions about moral questions, we have to set another characteristic of these questions which seems to contradict it. This is, that the answering of moral questions is, or ought to be, a rational activity. Although most of us think that we are free to form our own opinions about moral questions, we do not feel that it does not matter what we think about them—that the answering of moral questions is a quite arbitrary business, like the choice of one postage stamp from the sheet rather than another. We feel, rather, that it matters very much what answer we give, and that the finding of an answer is a task that should engage our rational powers to the limit of their capacity. So the freedom that we have in morals is to be distinguished from the freedom which comes when it simply does not matter what we do or say. That is why, when people grow up to the stage at which they start to understand that in moral questions they are free to form their own opinions, they feel this freedom not as an emancipation but as a burden.

This antinomy is the source of nearly all the central controversies of moral philosophy. Most moral philosophers have taken their stand on one side of it or the other, and this has left them denying important truths which are emphasized by the side which they have rejected. Some have thought it so important to preserve our freedom in moral matters, that they have denied the rationality of morals, because they thought (wrongly) that it was a restraint upon freedom. To this class belong most of those philosophers known by the highly ambiguous name of 'subjectivists', together with those others called 'emotivists'. Others have thought it so important to emphasize that moral thought can be a rational activity, that they have, because freedom appeared incompatible with rationality, denied our freedom to form our own opinions. To this class belong all those moral philosophers whom I shall call 'descriptivists', of whom the principal group are those called 'naturalists'. It is the task of moral philosophy, and the task of this book, to look for a way of reconciling these apparently incompatible positions, and thus resolving the antinomy between freedom and reason.

1.3. The key to the problem is the study of the concepts which have, through being misunderstood, brought us into this perplexity. This was my purpose in undertaking the inquiry whose results I published in my earlier book *The Language of Morals*.[1] In it I said 'It is not surprising that the

---

[1] References to *The Language of Morals* will take the form of the letters *LM* followed by the numbers of the chapter and section. References

first effect of modern logical researches was to make some philosophers despair of morals as a rational activity. It is the purpose of this book to show that their despair was premature' (*LM* 3.4). But it is necessary not merely to achieve an understanding of the moral concepts, but to use this understanding in order to give an account of moral reasoning—showing that moral arguments proceed as they do because the logical character of the concepts is what it is.

I shall not ask the reader to accept everything that was said in *The Language of Morals*. The argument of the present book fortunately does not require as premisses all the conclusions of the previous one. It does require, however, three main premisses which are to be found there, and which constitute the three most important truths about moral judgements. Of these, two are that moral judgements are a kind of *prescriptive* judgements, and that they are distinguished from other judgements of this class by being *universalizable* (*LM* 11.5). What these terms mean, and whether moral judgements are the only universalizable prescriptive judgements, will have to be discussed later. I shall be saying a good deal more in explanation and justification of these propositions; to that extent the argument of this book is independent of that of the earlier one. But, since I do not wish to repeat what was said in the other book, I must ask the reader to bear in mind that not all that could be said in support of these two theses is to be found here; the defences become much stronger when they have added to them the arguments of the previous book.

The third of these premisses I shall not argue for in this book at all, having already said enough about it. This is, that it is possible for there to be logical relations between prescriptive judgements, including even imperatives (e.g. imperatives can be in contradiction one with another). When I wrote my earlier book, I considered this to be the single most

without any preceding letters, or preceded by a semi-colon, are to chapters and sections of this book.

important element in a rationalist moral philosophy. That
was why I devoted the first third of that book to a discussion
of imperatives. If, as I believe, moral judgements are prescriptive, then moral argument cannot get any grip, unless
there are some logical relations between prescriptive judgements. I thought that the best way of showing that there are
such relations was to take the extreme case, commands, and
to show that there could be logical relations even between
these. In spite of several explicit disavowals, I have often been
accused of wanting to 'reduce' moral judgements to imperatives, or even to orders, or commands in a sense very much
narrower than that in which I was using the term (*LM* 1.1,
1.2, 12.4). My purpose was rather to show that moral judgements share *one* important characteristic with imperatives,
that of being prescriptive, but that this does not prevent there
being logical relations between them; and that therefore it is
not necessary, in order to erect a theory of moral argument, to
show that they are purely descriptive.

As we shall see, the first two of these premises bear a close
relation to the two sides of the antinomy mentioned earlier.
It is, most fundamentally, because moral judgements are
universalizable that we can speak of moral thought as rational
(to universalize is to give the reason); and their prescriptivity
is very intimately connected with our freedom to form our
own moral opinions (only those who are free to think and act
need a prescriptive language). I shall devote the first part of
this book, therefore, to elaborating these two theses. In Chapters 2 and 3 I shall explain in some detail what I mean by
saying that moral judgements are universalizable, and the
relation between this feature of them and the fact (emphasized
in *LM* 7.1 ff.) that, though prescriptive, they have a descriptive element in their meaning. In Chapter 4 I shall ask what
it is about our human situation which gives rise to the need
for a language in which prescriptive judgements (among them
moral judgements) can be expressed; this will give me an

occasion to say a little, though no more than is necessary for my argument, about the problem of the freedom of the will. I shall argue that it is because we are free agents that we need to ask prescriptive questions, and that the prescriptivity of moral judgements explains both why there should be thought to be a problem about moral freedom, and how to approach its solution. In Chapter 5 I shall discuss what has been thought to be the most serious objection to the view that moral judgements are prescriptive—namely the existence of cases in which people do what they think they ought not to be doing.

In the second and third parts of the book I shall use these concepts of prescriptivity and universalizability in order to expound the beginnings of a theory of moral reasoning; I shall not be able to take this very far—but far enough, I hope, to shed light on some quite practical problems of morality. I shall end with a discussion of a particular group of moral questions, those concerning race relations, on which, it seems to me, the theoretical views which I have put forward have some bearing. This will be an earnest of my serious concern with practical moral problems, which some have surprised me by doubting.

From these vague introductory remarks—perhaps, as they stand, incomprehensible—we must now turn to something more like business. And I think it best to begin with a point on which most moral philosophers, from Professor Stevenson to Dr. Ewing, would probably agree—namely the fact that moral judgements, whatever else they may do, have, as one element in their meaning, what has been called 'descriptive meaning'. It is hard to deny that this is so, but harder still to say what it means; and this is what we now have to attempt.

2 · DESCRIPTIVE MEANING

2.1. WHAT is it for a term to have descriptive meaning?
Without attempting to give a complete account of meaning in
general, I may perhaps be allowed to say that meaning of any
kind (so far as it is words that are said to have meaning) is or
involves the use of an expression in accordance with certain
rules; the *kind* of meaning is determined by the *kind* of rules.
It must be noted that in speaking of 'rules' determining the
meanings of expressions, I am not making out language to be
more inflexible than it is. The terms 'open texture',[1] 'family
resemblance',[2] and the like (striking and illuminating when
first introduced) were not long in becoming part of the patter
of the up-to-date philosophical conjurer. They express the
undoubted truth that the expressions of our language (especially its descriptive terms) are used very tolerantly; not only
is their use subject to change, but at any one time there will
be many border-line cases in which there is a certain liberty
of use; and there are many other linguistic liberties which we
do not need to discuss here. This point has, as we shall see,
some importance for ethics—though we must always be on
our guard against the temptation to take advantage of the
flexibility of language in order to blur philosophical issues. It
suffices for our present purpose to say that by 'rules' I do not
mean very simple general rules which can be formulated in
words (3.4), but, rather, that consistency of practice in the use
of an expression which is the condition of its intelligibility.

It is one of the commonest mistakes in philosophy (this is

[1] See Waismann, *Aristotelian Society*, Supp. Vol. xix (1945), 123, and
his series of articles 'Analytic-Synthetic' in *Analysis*, x–xiii (1949–53).

[2] See Wittgenstein, *Philosophical Investigations*, §§ 66 f., and other passages referred to by R. Bambrough, *Aristotelian Society*, lxi (1960/1), 207,
in a useful exposition of some of the lessons to be learnt from Wittgenstein's doctrine.

another piece of patter) to suppose that all rules determining meaning have to be of the same kind, i.e. that all terms have meaning in the same sort of way. The best method of distinguishing between different kinds of meaning-rules is to ask what, in the case of terms of different kinds, would constitute *misuse* of them. Let us therefore try this method with the word 'red', which I shall take as a typical example of a descriptive term. How should we be sure that a person had misused the word 'red'? We should be entitled to accuse him of doing this if he said that an object was red when what he meant was that it was of some other kind. The sense of 'meant' which I am using here is that in which *we* can mean something different from what *our words* mean in their correct acceptation (as when an Englishman in Italy says 'acqua calda' meaning 'cold water'). In the first sense what *we* mean is what we intend to convey; in the second sense what *our words* mean is what they would normally convey to somebody who understood the language which we are speaking.

In general, a person is misusing a descriptive term if in using it he breaks the descriptive rule attaching the term to a certain kind of objects; and he does this if he says that an object is of one kind, meaning, or intending to convey, that it is of another kind. A descriptive term may thus be defined as one, to misuse which is to do this.

In order to know that a person has misused a descriptive term we have to know what he meant, or intended to convey. In practice we normally get over this difficulty by making an assumption: that he intends to convey what is in fact true. This in turn splits up into two assumptions: we have to assume both that he is not honestly mistaken about what kind of thing the object actually is; and that he is not deliberately speaking falsely. If either of these assumptions cannot be made, it is very difficult to distinguish incorrect uses of descriptive terms from deliberate or unintentional false statements. For suppose that he says, of a blue object, that it is red.

Unless we make these assumptions, we cannot conclude that he is misusing the word 'red'—i.e. expressing incorrectly what he intends to convey. He may be using it quite correctly to express a false statement which he either thinks true or wishes to deceive us into thinking true. Fortunately these complications (which are in fact even more complicated than there is here room to indicate) need not concern us. If the two assumptions be granted, as they usually can be, we can detect a misuse of a term by observing that the term is used of an object of a certain kind, when the descriptive rule which determines the meaning of the term excludes its use of objects of that kind. Normally, if a man said that an object was ultramarine, when it was not, and when the object was in plain view, and he had normal eyesight, and was a straightforward person, we should conclude that he did not know the meaning of 'ultramarine'.

It might be thought that the same sort of thing can be said about all words; but, as I have said, to think this is to make one of the commonest of philosophical mistakes. In order to see that it is a mistake, it is necessary only to examine some expressions which do not follow this sort of meaning-rule. Take, for example, the word 'it'. The rules for the use of this word permit us to apply it to *any* kind of object or thing. If, therefore, it were a descriptive term, it would be so vague and general as to be altogether useless; by describing a thing as 'it' we should not be describing it at all. But in fact 'it' has an entirely different use from that of describing; it is used to *refer to* (not describe) something whose identity is already established by the context. If, for example, we say 'That's it', we are not describing *that* as *it*; we are, rather, saying that that is the thing referred to. What this thing is has to be clear from the context. For this reason it is not possible to misuse the word 'it' by using it of an object of a kind to which it is not correctly applied (for it can be used of *any* kind of object). Fortunately it is irrelevant to our purpose to inquire into the very difficult question of what *would* constitute a misuse of the word 'it'.

Having explained how the class of descriptive *terms* is to be defined, we can now go on to do the same for the class of descriptive *judgements*.[1] A judgement is descriptive if in it the predicate or predicates are descriptive terms and the mood is indicative. The latter restriction is required because imperative sentences also normally contain descriptive terms (for instance in 'Be quiet' the expression 'quiet' is a descriptive term); and we do not want to have to call imperatives descriptive judgements. I am using the word 'predicate' to cover not only what are sometimes called 'one-place' predicates but also predicates (such as relational terms) which can take more than one subject. Thus my account is intended to cover not only subject-predicate propositions in the narrow sense, but also relational ones. For example 'hit' is a two-place predicate, expressing a relation; the sentence 'John hit James' expresses a descriptive judgement because in it this two-place predicate, which is a descriptive term, is predicated, in the indicative, of the ordered pair of subjects John and James.

2.2. We must now notice the connexion between the fact that some judgements are descriptive and another feature which it has become the custom to call, when we are speaking of moral judgements, *universalizability*. It is important to emphasize that moral judgements *share* this feature with descriptive judgements, although the differences between them in other respects are, as we shall see, sufficient to make it misleading to say that moral judgements are descriptive. Nevertheless, in so far as moral judgements do have descriptive meaning, in addition to the other kind of meaning which they have, they share this characteristic, which is common to all judgements which carry descriptive meaning.

---

[1] I have used the term 'judgement', here and in *LM*, in an artificially general sense, in order to avoid subscribing to the fiction that all indicative sentences express statements, and in order to leave *some* questions unbegged.

If a person says that a thing is red, he is committed to the view that anything which was like it in the relevant respects would likewise be red. The relevant respects are those which, he thought, entitled him to call the first thing red; in this particular case, they amount to one respect only: its red colour. This follows, according to the definitions given above, from the fact that 'This is red' is a descriptive judgement. 'This is red' entails 'Everything like this in the relevant respects is red' simply because to say that something is red while denying that some other thing which resembles it in the relevant respects is red is to misuse the word 'red'; and this is because 'red' is a descriptive term, and because therefore to say that something is red is to say that it is of a certain kind, and so to imply that anything which is of that same kind is red.

The proposition 'Everything like this in the relevant respects is red' is not, indeed, formally and in the strictest sense a universal one; for it contains the singular term 'this'. But, as I have explained elsewhere,[1] when a singular term is governed by the word 'like' or its equivalent, it has the property of being turnable into a universal term by substituting for 'like this' a term which describes the respects in which the thing in question is being said to be like this. If no suitable word exists, it is always possible to invent one. And so if a person who says 'This is red' is committed also to the proposition 'Everything like this in the relevant respects is red', then he is, further, committed to the proposition that there is a property such that this has it and such that everything which has it is red. And the second part of this proposition contains no singular terms, and can therefore be called properly universal.

It may be observed that the proposition 'There is a property such that everything which has it is red' is a very trivial one, since the property in question is redness, and we know that there is such a property, once we know what sort of word

[1] *Aristotelian Society*, lv (1954/5), 307.

'red' is (i.e. a descriptive word). But note that there are in fact other properties such that everything that has them is red (e.g. the properties of being scarlet, or of being a ripe tomato of the commonest variety). We may admit, however, that, since this proposition, even if it were not non-trivially true, would still be trivially true, 'red' being the sort of word that it is, the thesis that descriptive judgements are universalizable is a quite trivial thesis. It is put forward here only because it will help us to shed light on the thesis, which is itself not so trivial, that moral judgements are, *in the same sense*, universalizable.

2.3. For the moment, however, let us merely observe that in an apparently trivial, but at any rate unobjectionable, sense, any singular descriptive judgement is universalizable: viz. in the sense that it commits the speaker to the further proposition that anything exactly like the subject of the first judgement, or like it in the relevant respects, possesses the property attributed to it in the first judgement. Let us now raise against this thesis some of the objections that are often raised against the corresponding thesis about value-judgements. First (it may be said) if, in the formulation of the thesis, we say 'exactly like', then the thesis becomes trivial and not worth stating. Nothing, it may be said, ever *is* exactly like anything else—whether this be regarded as analytic or not need not concern us. On the other hand (the objection goes on) if we say 'like in the relevant respects', we have on our hands the problem of how to determine and formulate what *are* the relevant respects. And if we cannot do this, it is alleged that the thesis is again valueless.

To this it may be replied, first, that it is wrong to take too narrowly utilitarian an attitude towards philosophical theses; let it suffice that they are true, and let it be left to the future to determine whether any useful results follow from them. Secondly, the thesis has indeed an important impact on the theory of meaning, just as the corresponding thesis about value-judgements has momentous consequences for ethics. The thesis enables us to illuminate the problem of what is meant by 'descriptive meaning'. This is not surprising; for we derived the thesis from a consideration of what it was for a term to be descriptive. One of the features of descriptive meaning, as opposed to other sorts of meaning, is that it relies upon the concept of *similarity*. We might restate what we noticed above about descriptive meaning by saying that a descriptive meaning-rule is one which lays it down that we may apply an expression to objects which are similar to each other in certain respects. It is a direct consequence of this that we cannot without inconsistency apply a descriptive term to one thing, and refuse to apply it to another similar thing (either exactly similar or similar in the relevant respects). At any rate a person who admitted that two things were exactly similar, but applied some descriptive term to one while refusing to apply it to the other, though he claimed to be using the term unambiguously, would be showing that he either did not understand that the expression was a descriptive term, or did not understand what a descriptive term was.

It thus turns out that the universalizability of singular descriptive judgements is a consequence of the fact that the meaning-rules for the descriptive terms which they have to contain are universal rules, and universal rules of a certain type. The difficulty of formulating precisely the respect in which the two objects have to be similar is simply the difficulty of determining the precise meaning in which the speaker was using the term. For example, suppose that I say that X is red; I am committed to holding that anything which is like X in the relevant respect is also red. But suppose that I am asked what *is* the relevant respect. I shall be able to answer this question only by giving an indication, vague or precise, of what it was about X that made me call it red; i.e. by explaining what I meant by calling it red. This explanation, if I can give it, will determine in what respect another object has to resemble X before it becomes possible to, and impossible not to, apply to it the descriptive term 'red', in the sense in which I was using that term. In this particular case an ostensive explanation (possibly a very elaborate one) will be required.

I must emphasize again that I am not making language out to be more rigid than it is. It is, of course, true that the concept 'red' is one whose boundaries are ill-defined. One man might call an object red which another said was not red—and that, not because there was a difference in their colour-vision, but because they had learnt to use the word 'red' in slightly different ways. Colour-cards from different manufacturers of paint often vary in this way; one card may, for example, classify as green a shade which is called on the other some sort of yellow. And a person might *change* his use of the word 'red' slightly; he might come to include in red, shades which previously he included in purple. The history of the word 'purple' itself illustrates this sort of change; the dye from whose name the word 'purple' is derived would now be classified by almost everybody as a red. All I am saying is that on any one occasion of the use of the word 'red' the speaker must have *some* feature of an object in mind as that to which he is drawing attention in using the word. He may be very unclear about the precise boundaries of the concept he is employing (we can use 'red' without having decided what we would say about border-line cases); but there must be *something* about the object in question which, if it were repeated. in another object, he would (provided that he went on using the word in the same sense) treat as entitling him to call that object red too. If this were not so, what he said would have no descriptive meaning at all. Thus (if I may be allowed to anticipate my future argument) the alleged difficulty of *formulating* the universal rule which is implied in any value-judgement is simply the same sort of difficulty which is encountered when we try to explain the meaning of a descriptive term as used on a particular occasion.

2.4. Let us now consider a further objection, also on grounds of triviality. It might be said that the universal proposition which is generated, in the way described above, by any singular descriptive judgement is merely a matter of the *meaning* of the descriptive term contained in the judgement; that it cannot be a matter of substance. If I say that X is red, I am committed to holding that anything which is like X in a certain respect is red too. In using the descriptive term 'red' I must be employing *some* universal rule; but, it might be objected, this rule is only that which gives the meaning of 'red'; it is a purely verbal matter of how the word 'red' is used. Now this I do not wish to deny, in the case of purely descriptive terms; as we shall see, evaluative terms differ in this respect. The universal rules which are involved in the use of all descriptive expressions are meaning-rules; and since these are obviously in some sense universal (in what sense, I have tried to make clear), it seems hardly worth saying that singular descriptive propositions commit the speaker to universal propositions. And perhaps in most philosophical contexts it would not be worth saying. But in the present context it is most important; for I am going on to speak about the universalizability of value-judgements (upon which a great deal hangs in ethics), and it is most necessary that it should be understood what I mean by this. The way which I have chosen of explaining what I mean is by saying that the feature of value-judgements which I call universalizability is simply that which they share with descriptive judgements; namely the fact that they both carry descriptive meaning. It thus becomes very important to elucidate accurately this feature of descriptive judgements.

If I call a thing red, I am committed to calling anything else like it red. And if I call a thing a good X, I am committed to calling any X like it good. But whereas the reason in the former case is that I must be using the word 'red' in accordance with some *meaning*-rule, the reason in the latter case is much more complicated. For a naturalist, indeed, it would not be any more complicated; for naturalists hold that the rules which determine to what we can apply value-words are simply descriptive meaning-rules, and that these rules determine the meaning of these words completely, just as in the case of descriptive expressions. For him, a value-word is just one kind of descriptive expression. We may go further than this; for a naturalist is not the only sort of 'descriptivist'—if we may use this term for one who holds that value-words are simply one kind of descriptive word. It is true also of non-natural descriptivists such as Moore that for them value-words are descriptive terms whose meanings are completely determined by the sort of descriptive meaning-rules that I have been discussing. The difference between natural and non-natural descriptivists is important for our argument. The non-naturalist holds that the feature which has to be present in a thing before a value-word can be applied to it is something which can be described only by using that or some other value-word; it is *sui generis*. On the other hand, according to the naturalist such a feature is also describable, though perhaps at greater length, in non-evaluative (usually empirical) terms.

2.5. For the sake of a name, let me refer to the type of doctrine which I put forward in *The Language of Morals*, and still hold, as 'universal prescriptivism'—a combination, that is to say, of universalism (the view that moral judgements are universalizable) and prescriptivism (the view that they are, at any rate typically, prescriptive). It will be useful to make clear at this point that it is not easy with consistency to attack both sides of the doctrine at once. For, as we have seen, it follows from the definition of the expression 'descriptive term' that descriptive judgements are universalizable in just the same way as, according to my view, moral judgements are. It is impossible consistently to maintain that moral judgements are descriptive, and that they are not universalizable. To put the matter even more starkly: a philosopher who rejects universalizability is committed to the view that moral judgements have no descriptive meaning at all. Though there have been, no doubt, philosophers who are willing to go as far as this, they certainly do not include many of those who have declared themselves against universalizability.

The matter can perhaps be made clearer in the following way. Let us call the thesis that moral judgements are universalizable, u, and the thesis that they are prescriptive, p. Now there are two theses about the descriptive character of moral judgements which require to be carefully distinguished. The first and stronger of these (d) is that moral judgements are a kind of descriptive judgements, i.e. that their descriptive meaning exhausts their meaning. This is descriptivism. The second and weaker (d') is that moral judgements, though they may possess other elements in their meaning, do have descriptive meaning. I wish to affirm p, u and d'. These three theses are all mutually consistent. As we have seen, d' entails u. p is consistent with d', because to say that a judgement is prescriptive is not to say that prescriptive meaning is the only meaning that it carries, but merely that it does carry this element in its meaning among others (2.8). Now, as I hope to show, the combination of p and u (or d') is sufficient to establish the rationality of morals, or the possibility of cogent moral arguments—it is important that p, as I shall show, so far from being an obstacle to establishing this, is actually a necessary condition for it (6.3, 9.4, 11.7). But there are those who think that they require for this purpose not merely the weaker theses u or d' but the stronger thesis d. Now d is indeed inconsistent with p; and therefore these descriptivists think it necessary to deny p. But, because p has been affirmed by myself and others in conjunction with u, and because the connexion between d' and u has not been noticed, u has perhaps acquired, in the minds of some descriptivists, a kind of guilt by association: 'Some wicked prescriptivists have affirmed u,' they seem to be saying, 'therefore it must be attacked.' But since *d*, which the descriptivists affirm, entails the weaker thesis *d'*, and this in turn entails *u*, it is impossible with consistency to affirm *d* and deny *u*. The major task of moral philosophy is to show how *p* and *u* are consistent. This task is not furthered by those who are so convinced that *d* is required as the basis of the rationality of morals that they reject out of hand *p*, because it is inconsistent with *d*; nor is it helped by those others who are so convinced of the truth of *p* that they reject *u* (which they wrongly think to be inconsistent with *p*). The subject will be understood when it is realized how *p* and *u* are both mutually consistent and jointly sufficient for establishing the rationality of morals; and that *d* is not only not necessary for this purpose, but actually prevents its realization, since it entails the abandonment of *p*, which, as we shall see, is an essential factor in moral arguments.

I shall argue shortly that a naturalist in particular cannot consistently deny the thesis of universalizability. But the non-natural descriptivist has, it must be allowed, a way of escape from this *argumentum ad hominem*. According to him, a word such as 'good', though descriptive, has meaning-rules which are logically independent of the meaning-rules of other, non-evaluative words. It is thus possible for him, if he wishes, to admit that moral judgements are, like other descriptive judgements, universalizable, but to admit this in such a trivial and innocuous way that he comes to no harm thereby, even if he wants at the same time to be, in substance, a particularist (if I may use that name for the opposite of a universalist). For suppose that we say to him: 'If you call *X* a good *Y*, you are committed to the judgement that anything which is like *X* in the relevant respects is also a good *Y*.' He can reply, 'Certainly; but the relevant respect is simply the possession of the *sui generis* non-natural property of goodness; an object might be like *X* in every other respect, and I could still refuse to call it a good *Y* if it had not got this property.'

Such a philosopher could indeed embrace, at any rate for all practical purposes, the extremest sort of particularism. He would be maintaining a thesis which is obviously false (for the reasons given in *LM* 5.1 ff.); but the argument which I have just put forward would not touch him. He could maintain a view similar in its effects to one attributed (wrongly, as we shall see) to the Existentialists by some of their British admirers: he could say that we have to examine every object in its uniqueness for the property *goodness* and other moral properties; and that by attributing a moral property to one object we are not committed to attributing it to any other object, however similar in other respects. Of course, if we find another object possessing just this property, we shall have to say so; but since this property varies quite independently of the other, non-moral, properties, this commitment is the reverse of onerous. Everything that the particularist wishes to say can be said—in substance—in these old-fashioned terms without denying anything that I have established in this chapter, provided only that he sticks to non-naturalism.

There is, it is hardly necessary to point out, another kind of non-naturalist who thinks (quite correctly) that moral properties do *not* vary quite independently of non-moral properties, but are in some sense consequential or supervenient on them. *This* kind of non-naturalist will be, so far as the present argument goes, in the same position as the naturalists.

For the naturalist, the way of escape which I have just described is not open. For he is wedded to the view that when we apply a moral predicate to an object, we do so in virtue of a meaning-rule which lays it down that this predicate can be applied to objects of a certain kind; and that the question 'What kind?' is answered, not by pointing to a *sui generis* moral property, but by indicating *other*, non-moral, properties of the object (including perhaps negative properties—for the *absence* of properties may be as relevant as their presence).

These are the properties which constitute *that* about the object which makes it a suitable subject for the application of this moral predicate. It follows that the kind of universalizability to which the naturalist is committed is not the relatively innocuous kind which, as we saw, the particularistically inclined non-naturalist can safely admit. For let us suppose that we are having the same argument as before, only with a particularist who wishes to be a naturalist. 'If you call X a good Y', we say to him, 'you are committed to the judgement that anything which is like X in the relevant respects is also a good Y'. He cannot, like the non-naturalist, while admitting this, claim that 'the relevant respects' are simply the possession of the *sui generis* non-natural property of goodness. They have to be, rather, some set of non-moral properties.

The effects, therefore, for the naturalist of his involvement in universalism are much more awkward for him, if he is inclined towards particularist views. For he is committed to the admission that, if he makes a moral judgement about one object, this must be in virtue of the possession by the object of certain non-moral features (*what* features is determined by the meaning-rule for the moral word in question); and that therefore any other object which possesses these features must also have the same moral judgement made about it. Thus it is quite impossible for a naturalist to be, consistently, any sort of particularist.

In the preceding paragraphs I have confined my attention, for the sake of simplicity, to the word 'good'. To avoid repetition, the reader who is in doubt as to whether the same remarks apply to other moral words is invited to go through the argument again, substituting other moral words for 'good', and confirming that it still carries conviction. For example, if 'right act' or 'wrong act' are substituted throughout for 'good object of a certain kind', all the same things can be said; and, in view of the very close connexion in meaning between 'ought' and 'right' and 'wrong', it will require only small modifications to carry through the same argument about 'ought'; this is clear from the fact that, for example, 'He ought not to do that' means the same as 'It would be wrong for him to do that'.

2.6. An illuminating way of approaching the thesis which I am maintaining (namely universal prescriptivism) is to look upon it as retaining what is sound in descriptivism (natural and non-natural), and adding to it an account of the other essential element in the meaning of moral judgements, the prescriptive. The truth in naturalism is that moral terms do indeed have descriptive meaning. It is not the only element in their meaning, and it is therefore misleading to refer to it, as do the naturalists, as *the* meaning of a moral term; but in virtue of possessing this descriptive meaning moral judgements are universalizable, and naturalism has the merit of implying this.

Another way of putting the point is this: both naturalism and my own view lay great stress on the fact that, when we make a moral judgement about something, we make it *because* of the possession by it of certain non-moral properties. Thus both views hold that moral judgements about particular things are made for reasons; and the notion of a reason, as always, brings with it the notion of a rule which lays down that something is a reason for something else. Both views, therefore, involve universalizability. The difference is that the naturalist thinks that the rule in question is a descriptive meaning-rule which exhausts the meaning of the moral term used; whereas in my own view the rule, though it is very analogous to a descriptive meaning-rule, and though, therefore, it is quite legitimate to speak of the 'descriptive meaning' of moral terms, does not exhaust their meaning (*LM* 7.1 ff). For a naturalist, therefore, the inference from a non-moral description of something to a moral conclusion about it is an inference whose validity is due solely to the meaning of the words in it.

The rule permitting the inference would be simply the descriptive meaning-rule for the moral term used, and to accept such a rule would be simply to accept a meaning for the moral word. Conversely, if the meaning of the moral word be once understood, there can, for the naturalist, be no departing from the inference-rule; it is impossible to refuse the conclusion of the inference without altering the meaning of the word. But for me the position is different. Since the 'descriptive meaning' of moral terms does not exhaust their meaning, the other element in their meaning can make a difference to the logical behaviour of these terms in inferences. This is the point at issue in the controversy about whether an 'ought' can be derived from an 'is'.

2.7. It is now time, therefore, to ask what effect the introduction of the additional, prescriptive element in their meaning has upon the logical character of moral words.[1] I shall not try at this stage to define the word 'prescriptive'. Its meaning will not become clear until much later. But let us start by supposing that we have a word which carries the descriptive meaning of some value-word, but lacks its prescriptive meaning. Such a word would be, in its logical character, just like an ordinary descriptive word. To know how to use it, we should have to know to what kind of things it was properly applied, and no more. Now let us suppose that we try to *add* prescriptive meaning to such a word, thereby, according to my theory, recreating the original value-word. Let us, to take the same example as I used in *LM* 7.2, coin the word 'doog' to carry the descriptive meaning of the word 'good' as used in the

---

[1] It must be emphasized that it is not part of my thesis that moral words are used prescriptively *in all contexts*; and it makes sense to call them 'moral' even when they are not so used. But on the prescriptive uses the other uses depend (4.2, 5.6 ff.; *LM* 7.5, 9.3, 11.3). 'Prescriptive' is to be understood here in a wide sense to include permissions (10.5). Thus the statement that an act is morally permissible is in this sense prescriptive. The logical relations between prescriptions and permissions are too complex to be dealt with here.

sentence 'He is a good man', without its prescriptive meaning. Let us first notice, as before, that the statement 'X is a doog man' will be universalizable. Anybody who makes it will be committed to the view that some man who was exactly like X, or like him in the relevant respects, would also be a doog man; and the relevant respects would be simply those which the descriptive meaning-rule for the word 'doog' specified.

Now what happens if we try to add prescriptive meaning to such a word? The inevitable consequence of such an addition is that the descriptive meaning-rule becomes more than a mere meaning-rule. Since our value-word 'good' is to be used with the same descriptive meaning as 'doog' the *content* of the rule will remain the same; but its logical character will change. The rule will still say that it is proper to apply the word 'good' to a certain kind of man; but in saying this (in enunciating the rule) we shall be doing more than specifying the meaning of the word. For in saying that it is proper to call a certain kind of man good (for example a man who feeds his children, does not beat his wife, &c.) we are not just explaining the meaning of a word; it is not mere verbal instruction that we are giving, but something more: *moral* instruction. In learning that, of all kinds of man, *this* kind can be called good, our hearer will be learning something synthetic, a moral principle. It will be synthetic because of the added prescriptiveness of the word 'good'; in learning it, he will be learning, not merely to use a word in a certain way, but to commend, or prescribe for imitation, a certain kind of man. A man who wholeheartedly accepts such a rule is likely to *live*, not merely *talk*, differently from one who does not. Our descriptive meaning-rule has thus turned into a synthetic moral principle.

This change brings other consequences with it. To illustrate them, let us consider the context of the words' use in more detail. I have so far been assuming that the society which is using these expressions 'good man' and 'doog man' has very inflexible standards of human excellence, and that therefore no question arises of the descriptive meaning of either word changing. But in the real world standards of human excellence change (for example, on the wrongness of wife-beating);[1] and therefore, if the expression 'good man' is to be used (as it is) to express changing standards, its logical character has to be such as to allow for this. This is done by making the prescriptive meaning of the word primary, and its descriptive meaning secondary.

It is not *necessary* that a value-word should be treated in this way. There are other moral words whose prescriptive meaning is secondary to their descriptive: for example 'industrious' (*LM* 7.5), 'honest', and 'courageous'. Let us imagine a society which places a negative value upon industry; there seem to be such societies in the world, in which the industrious man is regarded as a mere nuisance. Such a society could never (if it spoke English) express its moral standards by using the word 'industrious', like us, for commending people, only with a totally different descriptive meaning—i.e. commending them for totally different qualities, for example that of doing as little work as possible. If they did that, we should say that they had changed *the meaning* of the English word 'industrious'. The descriptive meaning of 'industrious' is much too firmly attached to the word for this sort of thing to be allowed; these people would be much more likely to use the word in its normal descriptive meaning, but neutrally or pejoratively; i.e. to give it no, or an adverse, prescriptive meaning.

But it is not so mandatory, though it is possible, to treat the word 'good', like the word 'industrious', as one whose descriptive meaning is primary (*LM* 7.5). If we came to disapprove of industry, we should not stop calling the industrious man industrious; but, if we had previously called him a good man

---

[1] See G. M. Trevelyan, *English Social History*, p. 65: 'But the "lordship" was held [in the fifteenth century] to be vested in the husband, and when he asserted it by fist and stick, he was seldom blamed by public opinion.'

because, among other virtues, he was industrious, we should, if we came to disapprove of his industry very much, stop calling him good. This is because the commendation which is the prescriptive force of the word 'good' is more firmly attached to it than any part of its descriptive meaning; we should therefore be likely to keep the word 'good' as a prescriptive word (part of our vocabulary of commendation), and alter its descriptive meaning.

It is useful to have in our language both secondarily evaluative words like 'industrious' and primarily evaluative words like 'good'; and we should therefore be suspicious, if any philosopher seeks to persuade us that we ought in the interest of concreteness to neglect the study of words like 'good' and concentrate on words like 'industrious' and 'courageous' (10.1). The object of such a manœuvre might be to convince us that *all* moral words have their descriptive meaning irremovably attached to them; but, fortunately for the usefulness of moral language in expressing changing standards, this is not so. To take this line would be to give an account of moral language which is, so far as it goes, true, but not sufficiently general (in the sense in which Newtonian mechanics is not sufficiently general). The account would suffice for the moral language of an irrevocably closed society, in which a change in moral standards was unthinkable; but it does not do justice to the moral language of a society like our own, in which some people sometimes think about ultimate moral questions, and in which, therefore, morality changes. Orwell's Newspeak in *1984* was a language so designed that in it dangerous thoughts could not be expressed. Much of Oldspeak is like this too—if we want, in the Southern States, to speak to a negro as an equal, we cannot do so by addressing him as a nigger; the word 'nigger' incapsulates the standards of the society, and, if we were confined to it, we could not break free of those standards. But fortunately we are not so confined; our language, as we have it, *can* be a vehicle for new ideas.

2.8. It must be noticed that the mere fact that the descriptive meanings of moral words can alter does not distinguish them from ordinary descriptive words. All words can alter their meaning; dictionaries are full of sub-headings which begin 'Obs.'. And even in the case of words in current use their meanings vary from occasion to occasion within at times quite wide limits. And there is 'family resemblance' and 'open texture' and all that. Some people have been misled into thinking that, since descriptive words have these features, and since what has caused a lot of the trouble with value-words is their shifting descriptive meanings, the trouble can be cleared up without distinguishing between the two classes of words. The premisses of this inference are perfectly true, but the conclusion misses the point. Value-words *are* indeed like descriptive words, both in that they have descriptive meanings, and in that the descriptive meanings of both are alterable, flexible, and so on. So, if we cared to concentrate on the resemblances between the two classes of words, and ignore their differences, we could call them all 'descriptive words', meaning by this 'words having descriptive meaning'. But to do this would be to neglect an important (indeed essential) part of the meaning of moral and other value-words; and the philosopher who wishes to do justice to this will have to be more careful in choosing his terminology.

The terminology to which I have myself tried to be consistent is the following. An expression which, in a certain context, has descriptive meaning and no other, I call a descriptive term, word, or expression, as used in that context; one which has prescriptive meaning (whether or not it also has descriptive meaning) I call a prescriptive term; and one which has both kinds of meaning I call an evaluative term. A value-judgement or evaluative judgement is a judgement in which such a term is used; on the other hand the mention of an evaluative term inside quotation marks, or similarly 'insulated', does not make a judgement evaluative. Not all moral judgements are value-judgements (*LM* 11.3). In *The Language of Morals* I used the words 'evaluative meaning' for the prescriptive meaning of evaluative expressions. This had some advantages, as being a less question-begging expression which did not presuppose that what gave these terms their evaluative meaning was their prescriptivity; but in the end it turned out to be in the interests of clarity to make this, in effect, true by definition (*LM* 11.2; 5.7); and so in the present context I feel at liberty to use the words 'prescriptive meaning' which do carry this presupposition, and are somewhat clearer in that they avow it. To give examples of the use of these terms: 'red', in most contexts, is a descriptive term (though not when used of communists by conservatives); 'good' is, as typically used, an evaluative term, and so are 'right' and 'ought'.[1] These terms are primarily evaluative; words like 'industrious', 'honest', and 'courageous' are, as explained above, secondarily evaluative. All words which are evaluative (whether primarily or secondarily) are also prescriptive; but there are expressions which are prescriptive but not evaluative (because they do not carry descriptive meaning as well). The ordinary singular imperative—or rather, to be strictly accurate, its 'neustic' (*LM* 2.1)—is of this kind.

Now the philosophers to whom I referred just now point out (rightly) that value-words are like ordinary descriptive words in that they both have descriptive meanings, which are, moreover, alterable and flexible in both cases. But the purpose of using the term 'evaluative' is not to deny that

---

[1] Some writers use the words 'evaluative' and 'value-judgement' in a narrower sense than this. They call judgements containing the word 'good' and some similar words 'evaluative' or 'value-judgements', and distinguish these from judgements containing the words 'right', 'wrong', 'ought', and the like, which they call 'normative judgements'. These two classes certainly need to be distinguished for some purposes, as we shall see; and this is a useful way of doing it. But since I have used the word 'evaluative' in its wide sense hitherto, it would be confusing to use it in a different sense from now on; I shall therefore continue to use it to cover 'ought' and 'right' as well as 'good'.

value-words have descriptive meaning; that is readily admitted, and arguments which seek to prove that they have descriptive meaning are not arguments against my position, which allows this. Nor are arguments designed to show that we can use the words 'true' and 'false' of value-judgements, or that we can speak of 'describing' somebody as a good man. We can say these things of any judgement which has descriptive meaning, provided that it is its descriptive meaning that we are adverting to. Nor do I wish to deny that the descriptive meanings of value-words are alterable and flexible; that this is so fits in very well with my thesis. I am not asserting that value-words are in this respect different from descriptive words. What I am asserting is that the character of what happens when the descriptive meaning of a value-word changes is profoundly affected by the fact that it has prescriptive meaning as well as descriptive.

This can be clarified by means of a simple example. Let us suppose (to use an example which is current) that two people differ in where they draw the line between a 'bush' and a 'tree'. It is possible to imagine situations (for example if bushes are to be cut down but trees left standing) in which such a verbal difference might lead to important misunderstandings. But these misunderstandings could be cleared up quite easily by means of an agreement on the use of the word. In agreeing to draw the line in a certain place they would not be settling anything except a question of meaning—a verbal question. Wherever the line is drawn, the same instructions as before can be unambiguously given: e.g. 'Cut down all bushes below 15 ft. high with the lowest branch less than 3 ft. from the ground'. So classifying something as a bush does not *by itself* entail a prescription to cut it down.

I wish to contrast such a case of purely verbal difference with a case of a *moral* difference, thereby showing that typical moral disputes are not purely verbal, as on a naturalist account they would be, provided that the non-moral facts were agreed.

Let us suppose that two people know all about the income-tax laws, and know, specifically, that a certain method of tax avoidance is perfectly legal; and let us suppose that they know all about the precise tax situation of somebody who is proposing to use this means of avoiding tax. One of them may say 'That would be wrong; it would be going too far; there are ways of avoiding tax that are morally perfectly legitimate (for example by claiming deduction on account of a dependent relative, if you have one); but this proposal goes beyond what I can condone'. But the other may say, 'In my view this proposal cannot be condemned on moral grounds; there *are* methods of tax avoidance which, though legal, I would condemn, but this is not one of them; in my view there is nothing wrong about it'. Now it is obvious that these two people cannot clear up their difference, as in the 'bush' case, by a verbal agreement to use the word 'wrong' to cover certain cases and not others (*LM* 3.5). It follows that the rules which these two people are using for determining the application of the word 'wrong' cannot be merely descriptive meaning-rules, although they do, among other functions, determine the descriptive meaning of the term. They are rules having moral substance; in accepting one or the other of them the disputants would be committing themselves, not merely to a certain use of a word, but to a matter of moral principle. So when we 'flex' our moral words, we have regard, not merely to matters of mere convenience in communication, but to substantial questions of morality.

3 · PRINCIPLES

3.1. I SOUGHT in the preceding chapter to explain in what sense moral judgements are universalizable. The explanation may be summed up as follows: they are universalizable in just the same way as descriptive judgements are universalizable, namely the way which follows from the fact that both moral expressions and descriptive expressions have descriptive meaning; but in the case of moral judgements the universal rules which determine this descriptive meaning are not mere meaning-rules, but moral principles of substance. In this chapter, I am going to consider various other ways in which moral judgements might be said to be universal or universalizable—mainly in order to avoid future misinterpretation by indicating to which of these views I subscribe and to which I do not.

It is, first of all, most important to distinguish the logical thesis which I have been putting forward from various *moral* theses with which it is easy to confuse it. I said above (2.7) that, because of universalizability, a person who makes a moral judgement commits himself, not merely to a meaning-rule, but to a substantial moral principle. The thesis of universalizability itself, however, is still a logical thesis. It is very important not to confuse the thesis of universalizability with the substantial moral principles to which, according to it, a person who makes a moral judgement commits himself.

By a 'logical' thesis I mean a thesis about the meanings of words, or dependent solely upon them. I have been maintaining that the meaning of the word 'ought' and other moral words is such that a person who uses them commits himself thereby to a universal rule. This is the thesis of universalizability. It is to be distinguished from *moral* views such as that everybody ought always to adhere to universal rules and govern all his conduct in accordance with them, or that one ought not to make exceptions in one's own favour. The logical thesis has, as we shall see, great potency in moral arguments; but for that very reason it is most important to make clear that it is no more than a logical thesis—for otherwise the objection will be made that a moral principle has been smuggled in disguised as a logical doctrine (10.3). In order to clarify this point I am going to take the two moral views just mentioned and show that they do not follow from the logical thesis, unless they themselves are interpreted in such a way as to be analytic (i.e. not to enjoin any one line of conduct rather than another). In the latter case, obviously, there would be no objection to deriving them from the logical thesis, because the accusation of smuggling in substantial moral principles could not then be raised.

3.2. Let us first consider the moral principle that everybody ought always to adhere to universal rules and govern all his conduct in accordance with them. The nature of this principle is best examined by asking what would constitute a breach of it. On one interpretation, it is impossible to break such a principle; for, given a description of a person's life, it is always, analytically, possible to find *some* universal rules according to which he has lived—if only the rule 'Live thus: . . .' followed by a minute description, in universal terms, of how he has lived.

To avoid this trivialization of the principle we are considering, let us stipulate that a man is not to be said to have *adhered* to a rule, nor to have *governed his conduct in accordance with* it, unless he has in some sense had the rule before his mind (at any rate from time to time) and unless his conduct has in some sense been motivated by the desire to conform to it. Now on this interpretation, a man would be breaking the principle that everybody ought always to adhere to universal rules, and govern all his conduct in accordance with them, if he did something on some whim without considering any rule involved in the action. Does it follow from my logical thesis that such a person acts wrongly? Not in the least, it would seem; for the thesis does not say that a person who maintained that one ought always, in this man's circumstances, to act as he did, would be committing any logical fault, and still less does it say that the man himself is committing any *moral* fault. If, on a whim, I give a blind beggar a coin, this does not, according to the logical thesis of universalizability, stop my action being right; for it may be that one ought always to give alms to blind beggars—or even that one ought always to give alms to them without reflection. I do not wish to argue for or against such rules, but only to point out that they do not contravene my logical thesis. A person who acted thus without reflection could not, indeed, be thinking that this was the right thing to do; for that would involve consideration (in some sense) of a rule or principle; but he could do the right thing all the same. In the same way, one may use a word rightly without thinking whether it is the right word; but if one does think whether it is, one has thereby raised a question of principle: Is this the way the word is rightly used?

Offences against the thesis of universalizability are logical, not moral. If a person says 'I ought to act in a certain way, but nobody else ought to act in that way in relevantly similar circumstances', then, on my thesis, he is abusing the word 'ought'; he is implicitly contradicting himself. But the logical offence here lies in the *conjunction* of two moral judgements, not in either one of them by itself. The thesis of universalizability does not render self-contradictory any single, logically simple, moral judgement, or even moral principle, which is not already self-contradictory without the thesis; all it does is to force people to choose between judgements which cannot both be asserted without self-contradiction. And so no moral judgement or principle of substance follows from the thesis alone. Furthermore, a person may act, on a number of different occasions, in different ways, even if the occasions are qualitatively identical, without it following from the thesis that all, or that any particular one, of his actions must be wrong. The thesis does not even forbid us to say that *none* of the man's actions are wrong; for it is consistent with the thesis that the kinds of actions he did in the kind of situations described were morally indifferent. What the thesis does forbid us to do is to make different moral judgements about actions which we admit to be exactly or relevantly similar. The thesis tells us that this is to make two logically inconsistent judgements.

We might conceivably interpret the principle that one ought always to govern one's behaviour in accordance with universal rules as simply a denial, *en bloc*, of all such self-contradictory conjunctions of moral judgements. So interpreted, the principle becomes, like all denials of self-contradictions, analytic. It does not make much difference whether we say that it is a second-order statement about the logical properties of moral judgements, or that it is a first-order, but analytic, moral judgement. It could be put in either of these forms without substantially altering its character.

The same treatment can be given to the principle that one ought not to make exceptions in one's own favour. If this is interpreted merely as a denial that it can be the case that I ought to act in a certain way, but that others in relevantly similar circumstances ought not, then the principle is analytic (a repetition in other words of the logical thesis), and no moral judgement of substance follows from it. But if it is interpreted to mean that a man who acts in a certain way, while maintaining that others ought not so to act, is always *acting* wrongly, then not only is the principle synthetic, but most of us would dissent from it; for the man may well be acting rightly, though the moral judgement that he makes about other people's actions is inconsistent with the judgement (if he makes it) that his own action is right. At any rate, the man's *action* cannot be a breach of the thesis of universalizability, although what he *says* may be; and this is what we should expect if, as I have been maintaining, it is a logical thesis and not a substantive moral principle.

I shall not go into detail concerning other possible moral principles which might be confused with the thesis of universalizability. Two famous ones may, however, be just mentioned. The first is the 'Golden Rule', if put in the form of a moral principle: One ought to treat others as one would wish them to treat oneself. If this were rewritten to read '. . . as others *ought* to treat oneself', then the same sort of account can be given of it as of the principles we have just discussed. By suitable interpretation, it can be made analytically true according to the universalist thesis; on other interpretations it becomes synthetic, but does not then follow from the thesis. If the word 'wish' is left in, the principle is obviously synthetic, and equally obviously does not follow from the thesis (6.9).

The second principle which may be mentioned is the Kantian one, which we may put in the form 'I ought never to act except in such a way that I can also will that my maxim should become a universal law'.[1] This, too, is capable of different interpretations; but it will be wisest, in a book of this character, while acknowledging a very great debt to Kant, to avoid becoming entangled in the spider's web of Kantian exegesis. If Kant is interpreted as meaning that a man who says that he ought to act in a certain way, but says 'Let others not act in this same way', is guilty of an implicit contradiction, then the Kantian principle is a way of stating a consequence of the logical thesis of universalizability. In this interpretation, *willing* (which is one of Kant's most elusive notions) is treated as roughly equivalent to *assenting to an imperative*, in the sense, not itself entirely clear, of *LM* 2.2. There is also a problem about the word 'can'; what I should wish to say

---

[1] Kant, *Groundwork of the Metaphysic of Morals*, 2nd ed., p. 17 (tr. H. J. Paton, p. 70).

about this will become apparent later (6.9, 10.4 f.). But it is a difficult enough task to make my own views clear to the reader, without trying to do the same for Kant's.

In general, I may anticipate my future argument by saying this: it looks at first sight as if we have a choice between two positions: (1) that the thesis of universalizability is itself a moral principle and therefore can have substantial moral consequences; and (2) that it is only a logical principle from which nothing of moral substance can follow, and that therefore it is useless for purposes of moral reasoning. It is the last clause ('it is useless . . .') which is here mistaken. Later, I shall try to show that, though the thesis is not a substantial moral principle but a logical one, and though, therefore, nothing moral follows from it by itself, it is capable of very powerful employment in moral argument when combined with other premisses (6.3 ff.). So the dilemma is a false one—though this has not prevented its being often used.

3.3. Having made it clear that universalism, as I am maintaining it, is a logical and not a moral thesis, I shall now try to remove certain sources of confusion as to its precise import. First of all, it may very well be asked whether this is a doctrine about *moral* uses of words only, or whether it is a doctrine about evaluative words in general.[1] The answer which I wish to give to this question is a somewhat complicated one, since we have to steer between at least two errors. It is a doctrine about evaluative words in general, but one which requires careful qualification. If we take as an example the word 'ought', it seems to me that, whatever the type of 'ought'-judgement that is being made (moral, aesthetic, technical, &c.) the judgement is universalizable (8.2).

This is one reason why the word 'ought' cannot be used in making legal judgements; if a person has a certain legal obligation, we cannot express this by saying that he *ought* to do such

---

[1] I must admit that what I said on this point in *Aristotelian Society*, lv (1954/5), 298, was worse than misleading.

and such a thing, for the reason that 'ought'-judgements have to be universalizable, which, in the strict sense, legal judgements are not. The reason why they are not is that a statement of law always contains an implicit reference to a particular jurisdiction; 'It is illegal to marry one's own sister' means, implicitly, 'It is illegal in (e.g.) England to marry one's own sister'. But 'England' is here a singular term, which prevents the whole proposition being universal; nor is it universalizable, in the sense of committing the speaker to the view that such a marriage would be illegal in any country that was otherwise like England. It is therefore impossible to use 'ought' in such a statement. The moral judgement that one *ought* not to marry one's sister is, however, universal; it implies no reference to a particular legal system.

It is even more necessary to distinguish 'ought'-judgements from ordinary *imperatives* in respect of universalizability. If, when the squad gets to the end of the parade-ground, the serjeant says 'Left wheel', this does not commit him (on pain of being accused of having changed his mind) to giving the same order, rather than 'Right wheel', on similar occasions in the future. But if, in a tactical exercise, the instructor says 'The situation being what it is, you ought to attack on the left', he will have changed his mind if, the next time this same exercise is gone through with a new group of cadets, he says 'The situation being what it is, you ought to attack on the right'. By 'changed his mind', I mean 'said something which is inconsistent with what he said before'.

Though, however, some philosophers have gone much too far in assimilating 'ought'-judgements (of all sorts) to simple imperatives, it may be that some people do sometimes use the word 'ought' when they should more properly have used a plain imperative, in order to give an instruction without any thought of reasons or grounds. Plain imperatives do not *have* to have reasons or grounds, though they normally do have; but 'ought'-judgements, strictly speaking, would be being misused if the demand for reasons or grounds were thought of as out of place—though the reasons need not be ulterior ones; some universal moral judgements already incorporate all the reasons they need or can have (*LM* 4.4).

Nevertheless, it may be that there is a debased use of 'ought' in which it is equivalent to a simple imperative (though I must confess that I have come across such a use only in the writings of philosophers). Just in case, however, there is such a use, it is convenient to put the matter in the following way: in by far the majority of judgements containing the word 'ought', it has the sense that requires them to be universalizable; there *may* be some peripheral cases where it does not have this sense; but at any rate in its *moral* uses (with which we are chiefly concerned) it always does. The word 'moral' plays here a far smaller role than I was at one time tempted to assign to it. It is the logic of the word 'ought' in its typical uses that requires universalizability, not that of the word 'moral'; the word 'moral' needs to be brought in only in order to identify one class of the typical uses, and that with which as moral philosophers we are most concerned. This means that the ambiguity of the word 'moral', which is notorious, need not worry us at this point. For in whichever of its current senses the word is being used, it suffices to exclude those peripheral uses of 'ought' (if they exist), in which it is not universalizable.

3.4. I now turn to the most serious of the misinterpretations to which universalism is subject. It is common to hear objection made to it on the ground that it implies that there are certain rather simple general moral principles which, in some unexplained sense, *exist* antecedently to the making of any moral judgement, and that all we have to do whenever we make such a judgement is to consult the relevant principle and, without more ado, the judgement is made. Such a doctrine would be that of a very hidebound moralist, whose moral principles were a set of copy-book headings.[1] This

[1] See further *Aristotelian Society*, lv (1954/5), 309 f.

account of the matter differs from that which I wish to give in a number of respects. First of all, it is not clear what is meant in this context by speaking of moral principles 'existing'; but even if they (in some sense) exist, I am sure that they do not always exist *antecedently*, so that all we have to do is to consult them. This is made sufficiently clear by considering almost any case of serious moral perplexity—for example Sartre's well-known case of the young man who was in doubt whether to join the Free French forces or to stay and look after his widowed mother.[1] Sartre uses the example in order to make the point that in such cases no antecedently 'existing' principle can be appealed to (*qui peut en decider a priori; aucune morale inscrite ne peut le dire*).[2] We have to consider the particular case and make up our minds what are its morally relevant features, and what, taking these features into account, ought to be done in such a case. Nevertheless, when we do make up our minds, it is about a matter of principle which has a bearing outside the particular case. Sartre himself is as much of a universalist as I am, in the sense in which I am, to judge by the little book in which this example occurs.[3] He has also on occasion himself given his public support to universal moral principles.[4]

Secondly, the principles which are adhered to in making moral judgements are seldom very simple or general, at any rate when the judgements are made by intelligent people who have had any wide experience of life. It is most important here to distinguish between what may be called *universality*

[1] J.-P. Sartre, *L'Existentialisme est un Humanisme* (1946), pp. 39 ff. (tr. in W. Kaufmann (ed.), *Existentialism*, pp. 295 f.)

[2] Op. cit., p. 42 (Kaufmann, p. 296); cf. p. 47 (Kaufmann, p. 298), where the point is the same.

[3] Cf. op. cit., pp. 31–32, 70–78 (Kaufmann, pp. 293, 304–6): 'I bear the responsibility of the choice which, in committing myself, also commits the whole of humanity'; 'In this sense we may say that there is a human universality, but it is not something given; it is being perpetually made'; '[The young man] was obliged to invent *the law* for himself' (my italics).

[4] See *The Times*, 21 Sept. 1960, p. 10.

and *generality*, although these terms are often enough used interchangeably. The opposite of 'general' is 'specific'; the opposite of 'universal' is 'singular'—though the existence of the term 'particular', contrasted with both 'universal' and 'singular', introduces complications into which we do not need to enter. It will suffice for our purposes if we explain the terms informally in the following way. It will be remembered that we explained the notion of universalizability by reference to the term 'descriptive meaning'. Any judgement which has descriptive meaning must be universalizable, because the descriptive meaning-rules which determine this meaning are universal rules. But they are not necessarily general rules. A descriptive meaning-rule says that we can use a certain predicate of anything of a certain kind. And it is obvious that in the case of some descriptive predicates we shall have to go into a great deal of detail in order to specify what kind—if indeed this is formulable in words at all. Let the reader try specifying exactly what he means by a word like 'primitive', even in some particular context, and he will see what I mean. He will find that in order to distinguish it from other words such as 'archaic', 'unsophisticated', &c., he will have to enter into a great deal of detail, and may end up by having recourse to examples. Yet these are properly universal predicates. Other expressions create somewhat different difficulties owing to their complexity; in order to define the word 'barquentine' it is no use saying that it is a kind of vessel, nor even a kind of sailing-vessel; 'barquentine' is a very much less *general* term than 'vessel'; yet both are, equally, *universal* terms. Now universalism is not the doctrine that behind every moral judgement there has to lie a principle expressible in a few general terms; the principle, though universal, may be so complex that it defies formulation in words at all. But if it were formulated and specified, all the terms used in its formulation would be universal terms.

If I make a moral judgement about something, it must be

because of some feature of the thing; but this feature may be one which requires much detail for its specification. It must be noticed that generality and specificity are, unlike universality and singularity, matters of degree. This enables us to put the difference between the two pairs of terms quite simply by means of examples. The moral principle 'One ought never to make false statements' is highly general; the moral principle 'One ought never to make false statements to one's wife' is much more specific. But both are universal; the second one forbids *anyone* who is married to make false statements to his wife. It should be clear from these explanations that the thesis of universalizability does not require moral judgements to be made on the basis of highly general moral principles of the copy-book-heading type. As I explained in *LM* 3.6 and 4.3, our moral development, as we grow older, consists in the main in making our moral principles more and more specific, by writing into them exceptions and qualifications to cover kinds of case of which we have had experience. In the case of most people they soon become too complicated to admit of formulation, and yet give tolerably clear guidance in familiar situations. It is, indeed, always possible for a situation to arise which calls for a qualification of the principle; but, unless a person is plunged suddenly into an environment quite different to that in which he has grown up, this is likely to happen less and less as he grows older, because the situations which he encounters will more often resemble ones which he has encountered, and thought morally about, before.

3.5. The logic of moral language is not restrictive with regard to the generality or specificity of our moral principles. It allows them to be highly general and simple, or highly specific and complicated, according to the temperament of the person who holds them. This may be seen by considering some extreme cases. There might be one man who acquired early in life a few very short moral prohibitions, and stuck rigidly to these, while regarding everything not falling under them as equally permissible. Another man might accumulate a series of moral principles as complicated as the Law of Moses (whether or not he could formulate them), and still be adding qualifications until his dying day.

There is a great difference between people in respect of their readiness to qualify their moral principles in new circumstances. One man may be very hidebound; he may feel that he knows what he ought to do in a certain situation as soon as he has acquainted himself with its most general features, without examining it at all closely to see whether it has any special feature which would call for a different judgement. Another man may be more cautious (some people are even pathologically cautious in this respect); he will never make up his mind what he ought to do, even in a quite familiar situation, until he has scrutinized every detail of it to make sure that he can really subsume it under the principles that seem at first sight most relevant.

If some British admirers of the Existentialists were to be followed, we should all be like the latter person; we should say to ourselves that people, and the situations in which they find themselves, are unique, and that therefore we must approach every new situation with a completely open mind and do our moral thinking about it *ab initio*. This is an absurd prescription, only made plausible by concentrating our attention, by means of novels and short stories, on moral situations of extreme difficulty and complexity, which really do require a lot of consideration. It is important to realize that there are moral problems of this kind; but if *all* moral questions were treated like this, not only should we never get round to considering more than the first few that we happened to encounter, but any kind of moral development or learning from experience would be quite impossible. What the wiser among us do is to think deeply about the crucial moral questions, especially those that face us in our own lives; but when we have arrived at an answer to a particular problem, to crystallize it into a not too specific or detailed form, so that its salient features may stand out and serve us again in a like situation without need for *so much* thought. We may then have time to think about *other* problems, and shall not continually be finding ourselves at a loss about what we ought to do.

3.6. We have here, as so often in philosophy, to steer between two mistakes. It is unfortunate that terminological confusions tend often to drive us into one or the other. The expressions 'moral principle', 'moral rule', and the like are often interpreted in such a way that the rules or principles referred to have to be highly general. There are two main ways of achieving this. One is that of confining 'principles', as so restricted, to a relatively minor role in our moral thought. A man may make most of his moral decisions on grounds or for reasons which, though falling under the definition of 'universal principle' that I have been using, are insufficiently general to be called 'principles' in the restricted sense. He may reserve this word for what he calls 'matters of principle' —as when we say 'I make it a matter of principle *never* to come between husband and wife'. The purpose of making something a matter of principle, in this sense, is to avoid doing any moral thinking about particular cases.

There are sometimes justifications for this. It may be that the situations falling under the principle are such as leave no time for careful consideration of their particular features. It may be that such consideration is thought of as itself wrong (as perhaps in the instance just quoted; we may feel that to delve into other people's marital relations, as would be necessary if we were going to form a just judgement on them, would be an intolerable piece of interference). Or it may be that we have learnt from experience that, while we are engaged in a situation of a certain kind, moral thought is subject to recurrent pitfalls which in the heat of the moment it is difficult to avoid. For example, our natural kindness of heart, or desire to avoid scenes, may lead us to decisions which we subsequently come to think wrong. Or, in cases where we are in authority, we may think that arguments for treating a particular case in an exceptional way can always be devised by the ingenious; and that for this and other reasons, if an exception is made in one case (even though, because it is a hard one, there are reasons for doing so) there will be no end to the exceptions that will have to be made in less deserving cases. To use a frivolous example from a recent broadcast programme: if the hotel manager allows the old lady to have her Pekinese on her lap in the lounge, then there will be no stopping people bringing in Great Danes and Wolfhounds and knocking over the tables; so he makes it a matter of principle to allow no dogs in the lounge.

A more serious example is provided by the question, whether it is ever legitimate to use torture in police interrogations. A police officer might determine as a matter of principle never to use it; and I should approve of his doing so. This is not, however, because I think it logically impossible that situations should arise in which, by a form of moral reasoning such as I can now accept (similar to that outlined later in this book), I could satisfy myself that torture ought to be used. It is in fact very easy to imagine such situations: suppose, for example, that a sadistic bacteriologist has produced and broadcast an infectious bacillus which will cause a substantial part of the world's population to die of a painful disease; and that he alone knows the cure for the disease. I should certainly not condemn the police if they tortured him to make him reveal it. But when I say that I approve of a police officer accepting it as a matter of principle not to use torture, I do not mean to deny that fantastic cases could be thought up in which it would be legitimate; what I mean is that, although a completely watertight set of moral principles covering all logically possible circumstances (if there could be such a thing, which is unlikely) would include a clause to allow an exception in such cases, it is unlikely to be possible in practice for a police officer (however intelligent and sensitive) to do the moral thinking which would be necessary to distinguish such cases from others, superficially similar, in which the principle forbidding torture ought to be adhered to; and it would be dangerous for him to try, because in the sort of circumstances in which torture is sometimes advocated and practised it is extremely difficult to think clearly and to consider all sides of the case. Moreover, in cases which actually occur—as contrasted with those which are logically possible —I hold, having seen the sort of things that happen, that the ill effects on society of this insidious evil are always such as far to counterbalance any good that might come of it, even if the most important consideration, the suffering of the victim, be left out of account. I have, therefore, no hesitation at all in saying that police officers, however desperate the circumstances, ought to make it a matter of principle never even to contemplate such methods.

The sort of consideration of hypothetical and fantastic cases which I have implicitly condemned is to be distinguished from that quite different use of hypothetical cases in moral reasoning which we shall later see to be both necessary and useful (6.8, 9.4, 11.7). It is always legitimate, in order to apply to moral argument the requirement of universalizability, to imagine hypothetical cases which really are, apart from the fact that the roles of the people concerned are reversed, precisely similar in the relevant respects to the actual case being considered; and this may properly be done, however fantastic the assumptions that have to be made, in matters which do not affect the moral issue, in order to make the hypothetical case seem possible. This perhaps holds even for people faced with urgent practical problems, provided that they have time to think at all; and most of us should, when we have time to think, think more about such matters. Indeed, there is nothing to prevent moral philosophers in their studies considering cases which fall outside even this limit—which, that is to say, are in their morally relevant particulars quite dissimilar from cases which are likely actually to occur. It may not be so useful to do this, as to consider cases in which the morally relevant features of actual cases are reproduced; but it may all the same be instructive. But for people in situations which expose them to a particular moral danger, it may some-times be best to put altogether out of their minds the possi-bility of exceptions to a principle. It is a very difficult matter to decide just when it is right to make something 'a matter of principle' in this way—it depends so much on the circum-stances and on the psychology of particular people. But we cannot say that it is never right.

We clearly do sometimes use the word 'principle' in this sense, though it should be equally clear that this is not the way in which I have been using it. Burke, strangely to our ears, uses the word 'prejudice' ironically in a favourable sense for the same kind of thing: 'Prejudice is of ready application in the emergency; it previously engages the mind in a steady course of wisdom and virtue, and does not leave the man hesitating in the moment of decision, sceptical, puzzled and unresolved. Prejudice renders a man's virtue his habit, and not a series of unconnected acts. Through just prejudice, his duty becomes a part of his nature.'[1] All but a few philosophers would commend a man for making some of his decisions in the way Burke advocates; but few of us (and probably not Burke) would think it right for *all* decisions to be made in this way.

Another, and less laudable, way of achieving generality in our moral principles is to treat them as a set of general maxims to which, in some sense (perhaps only verbally) we subscribe; we may as often as not, in our actual particular moral judge-ments, depart from them, but they form the background of our moral thinking (its mythology, we might almost say). Per-haps, though, a man whose moral 'principles' are like this is

[1] *Reflections on Revolution in France* (1815 ed.), vol. v, p. 168.

freed from the charge of hypocrisy (at the cost of incurring another charge of woolly thinking) by the fact that his principles are expressed in very vague terms, so that by judicious interpretation of them he can square his set of moral principles as a whole with any moral judgement that he finds himself making. As a practical guide to action such a set of principles has small value, because, at any rate in difficult cases, a wide variety of actions can be called conformable to them. Another expedient is to interpret the principles themselves strictly and precisely, but to adjust and vary (how?) the 'weight' which we give to them in particular circum-. stances. It is not, however, as a guide to action that such principles are attractive, but rather because they give a certain 'tone' to the moral life; a man can call himself a man of principle, while making his actual moral judgements in particular cases in the way that most of us do.

3.7. It is very easy, in revulsion from this caricature of moral thinking, to fall into the opposite error of abandoning principles altogether. Sometimes this idea is put in the form of a proposal to abandon *morality*; 'morality' and 'moral principles' and 'moral rules' seem somehow tainted; a young man, especially, may see in them the Victorian furniture that he has inherited from his grandparents, to be discarded as soon as convenient. This reaction is very understandable, and in itself praiseworthy. In so far as moral principles are thought of as something inherited and external—as not accepted by a man himself as a guide to his actions (with the responsibility for fitting them to new situations), they are dead things. The mistake lies in supposing that moral principles have *got* to be like this. The remedy for it is to be clear about the sense in which we are using the words; and I shall therefore now set out the way in which I think they can most helpfully be used, if we are to make morality again (as the military writers say) 'operational'.

First of all, let us be clear that a moral principle has not got to be highly general or simple, or even formulable in words, though it has got to be universal (in the sense already explained). Secondly, let us insist that a man is not to be said to accept a moral principle unless he is making a serious attempt to *use* it in guiding his particular moral judgements and thus his actions. These two requirements are, as will be recognized, the two central theses of this book—that moral principles have to be universal, and that they have to be prescriptive. The latter of them compels us to look for principles that we can sincerely adhere to ; the former insists that these should really be moral principles and not the *ad hoc* decisions of an opportunist. It will be seen in Chapter 6 how these two features taken together supply us with a most powerful lever in moral arguments. And this is the sort of principle that we all actually use in our moral thinking, the more so as we gain experience.

Let us consider for a moment what it is for a man to be *wise*—to be the sort of person to whom we naturally turn for advice when faced with a moral difficulty. The word 'wise' is obviously evaluative; we shall not, on reflection, call a man wise unless we agree with the content of the moral advice he has given us—after we have seen the consequences of carrying it out, or disregarding it. But what is it in a man which leads us to expect that we shall be able, after the event, to say that his advice was wise? If I were seeking for advice in such a situation, I should look first for a man who had himself experienced difficulties of an analogous sort to mine. But this would not be enough; for the quality of the thought that he had given to these situations might have been poor. I should look also for a man of whom I could be sure that in facing moral questions (his own or mine) he would face them as questions of moral principle and not, for example, as questions of selfish expediency. This means that I should expect him to ask, of his own actions, 'To what action can I commit myself in this situation, realizing that, in committing myself to it, I am also (because the judgement is a universalizable one) prescribing to *anyone* in a like situation to do the same—in short, what can I will to be a universal law?' (5.5, 6.2). If I could find a man whom I knew to have been confronted with difficult choices, and whom, at the same time, I could expect to have had the courage to ask moral questions about them (not, to use Sartre's words, to 'conceal from himself the anguish'[1] of universalization), then that would be the man whose advice I should gladly seek, if it were moral advice that I wanted. And I should not expect him to produce quickly some simple maxim; he would, no doubt, find it extremely hard to formulate in words any universal proposition to cover the case. But I should be sure that he would consider the particular case carefully and sympathetically in all its details, and after doing that try to find a solution to which I could commit, not only myself, but, as Sartre again puts it, 'the whole of humanity'.[2]

3.8. This is perhaps the best point at which to guard against another common misinterpretation of universalism. It is thought that a universalist must inevitably be a busybody; for if, as he maintains, a moral judgement about my own case implies a similar judgement about similar cases in which other people are involved, then must not a universalist be a person who is always passing moral judgements on other people, and is not this a pretentious and insufferable thing to do? But first of all, to make a moral judgement about somebody else's action is not necessarily to go about proclaiming to him and to other people that he has acted well or ill. It is possible, and usually tactful, to keep one's moral opinions to oneself. But this answer to the objection does not go deep enough. A more important answer is that all the universalist is committed to in making a moral judgement is to saying that *if* there is another person in a similar situation, then the same judgement

[1] Op. cit., p. 32 (Kaufmann, p. 293).
[2] Op. cit., p. 74 (Kaufmann, p. 305); see above, p. 38, n. 3.

must be made about his case. Since we cannot know everything about another actual person's concrete situation (including how it strikes him, which may make all the difference), it is nearly always presumptuous to suppose that another person's situation is exactly like one we have ourselves been in, or even like it in the relevant particulars. If the other person asks us for advice, what we shall do, if we are sensible, is to question him very carefully about his situation; and if, after this careful and sympathetic inquiry, it appears that his situation has a good deal in common with one which has faced us, or if we are imaginative and sympathetic enough to be able to enter into his situation even without such previous experience, then we may have something in the way of moral advice that we can give him. And this advice, though based on careful examination of the specific details of the case, will have to be such as we could give in *any* similar case.

3.9. I wish, lastly, to clear up a pair of more elementary confusions. The first is that of taking 'universal' to mean 'universally accepted'. A moral principle would be universal, in this sense, if everybody in the world subscribed to it. It will be obvious that at any rate not all moral principles are universal in this sense, since there is widespread disagreement about many important moral questions; and I hope that it will be equally obvious that it is not in this sense that I am using the word. In any case, it is far from clear what relevance it has for moral philosophy whether or not there are moral principles which are universally accepted; it seems to me that *securus judicat orbis terrarum* is a pernicious maxim in morals, because it combines the vices of relativism with a plausibly absolutist ring. But to discuss this would be to digress.

The second confusion is more difficult to clear up. Suppose that somebody argues as follows: according to the universalist, when a man makes a moral judgement he is committed to saying that anybody who says something different about a similar case is wrong; therefore, according to the universalist, toleration in moral matters is impossible. In order to understand this matter clearly, it is necessary to distinguish between thinking that somebody else is wrong, and taking up an intolerant attitude towards him. The universalist is committed to a denial of relativism (which is in any case an absurd doctrine);[1] he holds that if anybody disagrees with me about a moral question, then I am committed to disagreeing with him, unless I change my mind. This appears a harmless enough tautology, and need hardly trouble the universalist. But the universalist is not committed to persecuting (physically or in any other way) people who disagree with him morally. If he is the sort of universalist that I am, he will realize that our moral opinions are liable to change in the light of our experience and our discussion of moral questions with other people; therefore, if another person disagrees with us, what is called for is not the suppression of his opinions but the discussion of them, in the hope that, when he has told us the reasons for his, and we for ours, we may reach agreement. Universalism is an ethical theory which makes moral argument both possible and fruitful; and it enables us to understand what toleration is, as we shall later see (9.6).

[1] Relativism, subjectivism, emotivism, and other such doctrines (none of which I hold) have become so inextricably confused with one another in philosophical writings as to make the term 'objectivism'—which is used indiscriminately to contrast with all these views, in all of their many forms —totally useless as a tool of serious inquiry. The confusion is increased by supposing, as many do, that anybody who is not what I have called a 'descriptivist' cannot be an 'objectivist' and must therefore be a 'relativist' or a 'subjectivist' or an 'emotivist', or all three—which, or in what senses, is seldom clear. For a crude and elementary attempt to sort matters out, see my article 'Ethics' in *Concise Encyclopedia of Western Philosophy and Philosophers*, ed. J. O. Urmson.

4 · 'OUGHT' AND 'CAN'

4.1. WE have seen that one of the distinguishing features of evaluative, including moral, language is its prescriptivity, as typically used. In this chapter I shall be drawing attention to the reasons, in our situation as men, for our having a set of terms with this feature. These reasons are connected with the fact that we, unlike stones, have to make choices and decisions about what to do. If stones were able to talk and describe their environment, they would not require any prescriptive language, except in so far as even talking is an activity which can be done right or wrong, well or ill.

It is because I *can* act in this way or that, that I ask, 'Shall I act in this way or that?'; and it is, typically, in my deliberations about this 'Shall I?' question that I ask the further, but related, question, 'Ought I to do this or that?' Thus it is because they are prescriptive that moral words possess that property which is summed up, perhaps over-crudely, in the slogan ' "Ought" implies "can" '. If descriptivism were a complete account of evaluative language, this slogan would never have arisen. We shall see that imperatives also imply 'can', in the same sense of 'imply', and for the same reasons, as does 'ought'; and when we have understood those reasons, we shall have explained sufficiently what are the similarities between moral judgements and imperatives which make me call them both 'prescriptive', to distinguish them from ordinary descriptive judgements which do not have this property.

The position is not, however, quite so simple as the above remarks, and the slogan ' "Ought" implies "can" ' itself, might seem to indicate. For it is not universally true that 'ought' (let alone other moral words) implies 'can'; that is to

say, there are many uses of 'ought' in which it is by no means
inconsistent with 'cannot'. This gives us another reason for
distinguishing, as I have elsewhere and as I shall again below,
between different kinds of uses of these words (*LM* 11.2;
5.6 ff.).

4.2. Let us consider some examples. Suppose that I say
'I ought to go and see him, but I can't, because I don't know
where he is'. There need be nothing inconsistent in such a
remark; and yet there would be if 'ought' always implied
'can'. But there are, in fact, various ways in which 'ought' can
be, as it were, weakened, so as no longer to possess the property which makes 'ought' and 'cannot' disagree. It is important to distinguish between various ways in which this can
happen, because it sheds light on other topics besides that
with which we are at present concerned.

First, there are the cases mentioned in *The Language of
Morals*: I may be meaning by 'I ought to go and see' merely
that there is, as a matter of sociological fact, a moral convention that people in my circumstances should go and see the
man in question; or I may be thinking simply that I have, or
shall have, as a matter of psychological fact, feelings of guilt,
remorse, &c., for not seeing him. So used, 'ought' by no
means implies 'can'; for in many cases people are unable to do
what moral convention requires, and in many cases they feel
guilt or remorse for their failure to do actions which they
know to have been impossible. That it is irrational to have
these feelings is beside the point; Jocasta was not stopped
from hanging herself by the thought that her 'crime' was
fated. Neither is it true that if one has been unable to observe
a moral convention, one has not broken it; Jocasta had certainly broken Greek moral conventions by marrying her son
Oedipus.

In these cases, 'ought' fails to imply 'can' because it is not
prescriptive in meaning at all; that is to say, it is consistent
with its meaning, as used in this context, not to be intended

to serve as a guide to anybody's actions. But these are not, perhaps, the most interesting or the commonest cases. Commoner are instances in which a man who says 'I ought but I can't' is, indeed, prescribing and seeking to guide conduct, but falls short of intending a *universal* prescription which would apply to his own case. He is, that is to say, prescribing in general terms, but exempting himself because of the impossibility, in his case, of obeying this general prescription.[1] This kind of quasi-universal prescription is, as we shall see, very characteristic of our actual moral language (5.6). I have argued that moral judgements, when intended seriously and with their full force, must be taken as committing the speaker to some universal judgement applying to anyone in a relevantly similar situation. As we shall see, there are various declensions which, to match the human weakness of their users, moral judgements commonly undergo; and the most important of these is where a corner of the net is, as it were, lifted to allow the speaker himself to escape. I prescribe, that is to say, for everyone in such and such a situation, *except myself*; in my own case, I substitute for the prescription something weaker.

We have here an excusable example of such a declension. When I say 'I ought but I can't', I am prescribing in general for cases like mine; I certainly think that a man in my situation ought, *if he can*, to do the act in question; but the prescription fails to apply in my case because of the impossibility of acting on it. It is as if I said 'If I were able, it would be the case that I ought (full force); but since I am not able, that lets me out'.

4.3. The sense of 'imply' in which 'ought' implies 'can' is not that of logical entailment. It is a weaker relation, analogous

---

[1] 'Ought' will, however, even in this case retain its descriptive meaning, and thus remain universalizable, though the *prescription* implied in it is not universal; hence these remarks are consistent with 3.3. The word 'general' is used here, not (as in 3.4) in the sense opposite to 'specific', but in that in which we say that a rule holds in general, but not universally: i.e. it has exceptions.

to that which Mr. Strawson has claimed to exist between the statement that the King of France is wise, and the statement that there is a King of France.[1] If there is no King of France, then the question whether the King of France is wise does not arise. And so, by saying that the King of France is wise, we give our hearers to understand that we think, at least, that the question arises to which this is one possible answer, and that, accordingly, there is a King of France. And similarly, if we say that somebody ought to do a certain thing, and 'ought' has its full (i.e. universally prescriptive) force, then we give our hearers to understand that we think that the question arises to which this is a possible answer, which it would not, unless the person in question were able to do the acts referred to.

Now it must be noticed that imperatives also imply 'can' in the same way as 'ought' does when used with its full force. If I tell or ask someone to do something (whether by way of advice, request, instruction, order, or even prayer does not matter), I give him to understand that I think that the question to which I have given him an answer arises—i.e. that a decision is open to him. It would not do to tell a soldier to pick up his rifle if it were fixed to the ground. And the question which has to arise, if either a decision or the utterance of an imperative is to be in point, is the question which a man is asking himself when he is wondering what to do—the question that is answered, either when one tells someone else what to do, or when he decides for himself. Let us call this kind of question a *practical* question.[2]

The answer to the question 'What shall I do?' is not normally expressed in words when the agent answers it, though it is (in the imperative) when someone else answers it by way of

---

[1] P. F. Strawson, *Mind*, lix (1950), 330 (also in *Essays in Conceptual Analysis*, ed. A. Flew, p. 34). See also Collingwood, *Essay on Metaphysics*, pp. 38 ff.

[2] The phrase 'wondering what to do' is a translation of Aristotle, *Nicomachean Ethics*, 1113ª5; and 'practical' is derived from the word there used for 'do'.

instruction, advice, &c. Instead, the agent just acts (hence Aristotle's doctrine that the conclusion of a practical syllogism is an action).[1] But in order to discuss, metalinguistically, the logic of the answer that the agent gives (without which it is impossible to give a satisfactory account of moral reasoning) we shall require an expression in words of what he leaves unuttered. I shall later use for this purpose the form 'Let me do *a*'—though this has also other and commoner uses. A man who is wondering, in a game of chess, what move to make, may say to himself 'Let me try moving Q to KB 4', and act accordingly. It is in this sense that I shall be using this form of expression—in the sense, that is, in which it is the first-person analogue of the second-person 'Try moving . . .' and the first-person-plural 'Let's try moving . . .', and not in that in which it is the equivalent of 'Allow me to try . . .'. The uncommonness of this use is explained by the fact that, as Aristotle implies, we usually act without saying anything to ourselves. This is not the only case in which a thought's logical character and relations can be made clearer by expressing it in words, though normally it is not so expressed—enthymemes provide another example.

We may, then, give the following account of the reason why decisions and imperatives 'imply "can" '. They are both answers to practical questions—and sometimes (though not always) the fact that a man cannot but do what he is going to do stops any practical question arising for him; and therefore there is no place for a decision or an imperative. We shall have later to discuss the difficult question, just when this is so and when it is not. This is one of the central issues in the 'problem of free will'. But for the moment I am content to have established this important analogy between 'ought' and imperatives and decisions; they all imply 'can' for the same reason, that without 'can' a practical question cannot arise.

I ask the reader to note carefully that I have not said that

---

[1] *Movement of Animals*, 701^{a}7 ff.

'ought' itself is used in giving answers to practical questions, in the narrow sense just explained. The question to which 'ought' gives an answer is not that asked by a man who is wondering what *to* do, but that asked by a man who is wondering what *he ought* to do. These are different questions; and to keep them distinct I shall confine the term 'practical question' to the former, and use the wider term 'prescriptive question' to cover both it and the 'ought'-question, when that is prescriptive. The two questions are nevertheless related, in the following way: unless the practical question arises, the 'ought'-question cannot arise, if 'ought' has its full force (as it must have, if it is to imply 'can'). And the reason for this is that, when the word is being used in this way, its function is to offer help and guidance in answering the practical question (though not directly to answer it); and so, naturally, there is no point in asking the 'ought'-question when the practical question does not arise.[1] Thus the prescriptivity of 'ought', when so used, serves both to account for the commonly accepted notion that 'ought' implies 'can', and to discriminate the cases where this is indeed so from those in which it is not. There is, therefore, an important similarity and relation between 'ought' and decisions and imperatives, which distinguishes them all from ordinary descriptive judgements. We have already seen that there is also another important and contrary analogy between 'ought' and *descriptive* judgements, which distinguishes both of them from imperatives and decisions—namely that 'ought' is universalizable and they are not. It is the existence of both these analogies, and the need to keep them both in focus at the same time, which makes moral philosophy so difficult and so fascinating a subject.

4.4. We have next to discuss in more detail what could be meant by the puzzling phrase 'the question arises whether . . .'. As we shall see, it is disputable whether the phrase 'the question arises' is the happiest one for the concept we are

[1] See further *Aristotelian Society*, Supp. Vol. xxv (1951), 205 f.

employing; but, since it has acquired a certain currency, I shall continue to use it.

There are many things that might be meant by this phrase. First of all, it might mean that the answer to the question was *not already obvious or known*. We might say 'The question simply does not arise whether Jones is trustworthy; he obviously is not'. It is clear that this is not the sense with which we have to deal. Secondly, it might mean that the question is *actually raised by somebody*; we might say 'Yesterday, in the Finance Committee, the question arose whether Jones was being paid enough'. This sense is subdivisible into three, according as we mean by 'raised', that somebody asked it out loud; or that somebody, without saying anything out loud, let the words of the question pass through his mind; or that somebody, without putting the question into words even mentally, wondered whether something was so or not. As an example of the last case, suppose that I see the flash of a mortar, apparently fired in my direction; I may, in an intelligible sense, wonder whether I shall be hit, or whether to duck beneath the parapet, although there is no time for any words to pass through my mind. It is clear that these senses, too, are irrelevant to our discussion; for, to use the previous example, by saying that the question whether the King of France is wise does not arise if there is no King, we mean more than that nobody is actually raising it.

By saying that a question arises, we seem sometimes to mean that it *could* be raised; the difficulty is to interpret the word 'could'. We might mean by it 'could be actually uttered,' whether out loud or mentally; but with this sense we cannot be concerned, since it is always possible, provided that one has learnt to talk, and is not gagged or the victim of aphasia, to *utter the words* 'Is the King of France wise?' in a questioning tone of voice, and even easier to let these words pass through one's mind. We seem to mean, rather, something like 'could appositely, appropriately, reasonably, significantly, or comprehensibly be raised'; and it is very important here to distinguish exactly which of these things, if any, we mean, and in what sense. There are clearly cases in which it would be inappropriate or inapposite to ask a question, but in which, nevertheless, it arises, in the sense we are after. For example, if we were in audience with the King and discussing some momentous question of state, it might be highly inappropriate —indeed downright impertinent—to ask whether he was wise; but it might still be said that the question, in the required sense, arose. At least, it would seem that if we are to use this phrase for the concept which is relevant to our discussion, we shall have to say this (even if the phrase is not entirely a happy one); for it is commonly said that if the question does not arise whether the King is wise, then it is neither true nor false that the King is wise; but in the case just mentioned it might be true that he was wise.

Here, as in so many other places in philosophy, it is very important to distinguish between things which it would be ridiculous, inapposite, inappropriate, or even misleading to say, and things which would be false or incomprehensible or inconsistent. It is only when it would be false or incomprehensible or inconsistent to say something that philosophers should be professionally interested. For example, it has been correctly maintained that, in a normal case, to say of something 'It looks red' when one *knows* it to *be* red is to speak misleadingly, and that such a remark is inapposite and inappropriate. But not so much can be argued from this as has been thought; for it tells us little about the logical properties of the propositions 'It looks red' and 'It is red'. What little it tells us, it tells us in virtue of a general rubric which applies to all speaking, that it is often misleading to say something weaker when one is in a position to say something stronger. That this is a case falling under this rubric shows that in some sense 'It looks red' is a weaker statement than 'It is red' —but that is all. For, though misleading and inappropriate, it may be perfectly comprehensible and indeed true to say of a thing which one knows to be red that it looks red. And while there may not be any point, on most occasions, in saying 'It both looks and is red', it is not inconsistent or incomprehensible. And it is the inconsistency or incomprehensibility or falsity of some utterance on some occasion that tells us about the logical properties of the words used—not mere misleadingness or inappropriateness.[1]

In our present case similar considerations apply. The sense in which we require to use the phrase 'The question arises whether the King of France is wise', if it is to help us in our discussion, is the following: a question arises if, and only if, supposing that somebody did ask it (i.e. utter the words), it would be comprehensible what he was asking. Note that the 'what' here is an indirect interrogative (*quid*), and not a relative (*quod*). The point is that, for a question to be said to arise in the required sense, it must be the case that, if asked, we should be able to understand it in the sense, not merely of knowing what the words mean in their normal acceptation, but of not being driven to ask, with an air of bafflement, 'What on earth is being asked?' If a question is, in a certain situation, incomprehensible in this sense, then it does not (in the sense required) arise in that situation.

4.5. Let us now illustrate the way in which the impossibility, or the inevitability, of doing something stops the question of whether to do it arising. Suppose, to adapt an example of Aristotle's,[2] that I am in a boat sailing in the English Channel, and that it is fair weather. I can then ask 'Shall I land in France?', and this can be a practical question; somebody can say, by way of advice, 'Yes, land in France; we can get a good meal in Dieppe'. But suppose, on the other hand, that I am being driven on the French shore by a gale and that

---

[1] Cf. H. P. Grice, *Aristotelian Society*, Supp. Vol. xxxv (1961), 124 ff.

[2] *Nicomachean Ethics*, 1110ª3.

it is obvious that whether I shall land in France is out of my control; then, if I ask 'Shall I land in France?' this cannot be understood as a practical question, but only as a request for a prediction, equivalent to 'Am I as a matter of fact going to land in France?' Sometimes the very form of words makes it impossible to understand a question as a practical one; for example, it is clear that 'Shall I *be driven* on the French shore?' could not be a practical question. The reason is that the event referred to is described in such a way that it could not be the subject of a decision, order, request, or piece of advice, and therefore could not, either, be the subject of a question which asks for these things. Similar questions are 'Shall I fall downstairs by accident?' and 'Shall I go to the wrong room by mistake?' We cannot ask these questions comprehensibly, because the answers to them would be incomprehensible. If somebody said 'Fall down the stairs by accident' or 'Go to the wrong room by mistake', we should be at a loss to know what he was telling us to do, and should have to look for peculiar senses in which to take his words (as, e.g., by understanding 'by mistake' to mean '*pretending* to have made a mistake').

These illustrations could also be used to show that, in similar circumstances, an 'Ought I?' question would be equally incomprehensible, provided that 'ought' was alleged to be being used with its full force. When the word is being so used, it is impossible to understand what a man could be asking if he says 'Ought I to be driven on shore by the gale?' or 'Ought I to fall downstairs by accident?' or 'Ought I to go to the wrong room by mistake?' Here again, there are contrived interpretations that would make sense of these utterances; for example, the man might mean 'Ought I to be the sort of man who makes this kind of mistake; ought I not rather to take a course in Pelmanism to correct my absent-mindedness?'; but this need not concern us. It seems to be true in general that if a description of an action is such as to rule out a practical 'Shall I?' question, then it will also rule out, for the same reason, the corresponding universally prescriptive 'Ought I?' question. It is, in fact, the impossibility of deliberating, or wondering, whether *to* do a thing which rules out asking whether one *ought* to do it.

4.6. I am not so ambitious as to hope, in this short chapter, to solve any of the tangle of problems that go under the name of 'the problem of free will'. Anyone who thinks that he can clear up these problems in less than a complete closely reasoned book shows himself unaware of their complexity. My aim is the more modest one of showing how the fact of moral freedom is what gives moral language one of its characteristic logical properties; it is because we have to make decisions that we have a use for this sort of language. Nevertheless, what has been said so far does perhaps suggest a useful approach to the traditional problem, which it will be worth a digression to explain.

It is commonly thought that if human actions can be predicted, and especially if they can be predicted by means of 'causal' laws, then it is impossible to make moral judgements about them. This, indeed, is one of the chief sources of philosophical perplexity about free will. The perplexity might perhaps be lessened if we could establish that it is only in a certain class of cases that predictability rules out moral judgement, and that the mistake is to assimilate all cases to these. If we had a clear way to distinguish these different cases from one another, the problem would become easier. And it is possible that such a criterion is provided by the test 'Does the question "What shall I do?" arise for the agent?'

This test serves, at any rate, to distinguish from each other the clear cases, in which nearly all of us would be inclined to say, either that predictability ruled out moral judgement, or that it did not. In the case just described of the man who is wrecked on the French coast, we have a clear case where the predictability of the event makes it impossible to ask a prescriptive moral question. Let us contrast this case with another in which this seems not to be so. Suppose that there are two cashiers, one of unexampled probity and the other the reverse, and that the dishonest one says to the honest one, 'You need some money for your holiday; why not take it out of the till?' Now it might be possible for someone who knew this honest man to predict with certainty that he would reject the suggestion—with as much certainty, that is to say, as any contingent event can be predicted. We may even suppose that, with advances in neurology, it may become possible to examine such a man's brain with an encephalograph and predict on the basis of an assured scientific law that nobody with a brain so formed will ever steal money from the till in this man's circumstances. But this does not make me want to stop saying that the man does as he ought—and I must ask the reader whether he does not agree with me. The reason why this case is different from the 'gale' case seems to be the following. In the 'gale' case there was no question of the man asking himself 'Shall I be wrecked?' or 'Ought I to be wrecked?' if these are understood prescriptively. But in the 'cashier' case these questions not only arise—what the man does depends on what answers he gives to them. He actually considers the question 'Shall I take the money?'—he must consider it, since he understands the other man's suggestion, and rejects it; one cannot even reject a suggestion that one has not, at any rate for a moment, considered. And *if* he were to answer, 'Yes, I'll take the money', then he would take the money; only it is predictable that he will not give this answer.

The same can be said about the 'ought'-question. The question 'Ought I to take the money?' certainly arises for him; only he unhesitatingly and predictably answers, 'No, I ought not'; and it is because he gives this answer that he acts as he does. It would be absurd to say that because it was predictable that these questions would arise for him and that he would answer them in a certain way and act accordingly, therefore the questions did not really arise; this contains a manifest contradiction.

There are those who say that if, with the progress of science, we come to be able in principle to predict any action, we shall have to give up making moral judgements. We may suggest that they have perhaps been misled by the apparent analogy between cases of the 'gale' type and cases of the 'cashier' type. The real difficulties of the subject, however, arise when we take what seem to be intermediate cases, and try to decide to which of the two extreme cases, if either, they are to be assimilated. There is a great variety of cases which seem to be like neither of these—both cases which occur normally, and cases, such as those which are the result of post-hypnotic suggestion or brain-surgery or mental disease, where there are abnormal factors at work. So various are these cases, even within a single class (e.g. the hypnotic), that the proper discussion of them would take us too far away from our subject. I am reasonably sure, however, that if we are clear about the extreme cases, and are not misled by the analogy between them into espousing the naïve kind of determinism which says 'All is predictable; therefore moral judgements are out of place', we shall be able to avoid the more elementary confusions.

4.7. The absurdity of what I have called the naïve determinist view can be seen if we ask what a person who accepted it could possibly do about it—how it could affect his actual behaviour, linguistic and other. This question is best examined in the context of moral education, which so often illuminates questions in moral philosophy. Even if naïve determinism were true, it would not alter the position that we find ourselves in when we are trying to bring up our children. So long as people go on having to make up their minds what to do, they will have need of principles (including moral principles) to help them to do it. So long, therefore, as we know that our children will have in the course of their lives to make up their minds on questions which make a great difference to their own and other people's futures, we shall seek to give them, during their upbringing, something by way of a moral outlook which will help them in making these choices. The fact that the whole process was predictable—or even, for that matter, actually predicted by some clever psychologist, provided that he kept quiet about his predictions—would make no difference to our situation. If a naïve determinist were to come to us and say that we need not take any trouble with our children's education, because what they are going to do in the course of their lives is in principle predictable, we should be unlikely to take his advice. For even if our children's actions are in principle predictable, *we* do not know what they are going to be (if we did know, we might change our methods of education, and thus falsify the prediction).

If it is suggested that, because naïve determinism is true, we cannot but educate them as we are going to, then it must be answered that in that case the acceptance of naïve determinism can make no difference to us in any case. But it is to be doubted whether this follows from the doctrine; for according to it, presumably, the acceptance of determinism is as capable of determining our behaviour as any other stimulus. Let us therefore suppose that, as is manifestly the case, we are left, by the acceptance of the determinist doctrine, in the position of having to decide how to bring up our children; and let us ask what changes in our methods we might be led to introduce.

I have said that, even if our children's futures are in principle predictable, *we* do not know what they are going to be. But whatever they are going to be, one of the causes of their being as they are will be the sort of education which we provide. If the determinist were able to produce, at birth, a kind of horoscope predicting all a child's future conduct, then we might give up the task of educating the child. But this is in principle impossible, since one class of data which the determinist requires in order to compile his predictions consists in the environmental influences which affect the child in its formative years. If, therefore, on his advice, we were to abandon or alter the child's education, this part of the data would be altered, and the predictions would then be based on false data and therefore themselves possibly false.

We may conclude that that very large part of morality which is concerned with the education of children would not be rendered futile, though its content and methods might be altered, by any logically possible advances in the predictive power of psychology. But education is continued by self-education (*LM* 4.3). It would therefore seem that, if a person is trying to build up for himself a body of moral principles which becomes more solid as his experience of life increases, his endeavour is no more rendered futile by advances in psychology than is that of a parent who is helping his children along the earlier stages of the same process. For example, suppose that I am devoting thought to the question of whether one ought ever, through the possession of inherited wealth, to take for oneself advantages which the less fortunate cannot have (a serious enough question, partly similar to one which we know occurred to Wittgenstein, and which he answered in the negative); even if somebody else can predict what conclusion I shall come to, and on what principle I shall act (whether I shall give all my money away or not), this does not in the least absolve me from considering the question and making up my mind about it. For I have to act in *some* way, and therefore have to answer the question, 'What shall I do?'; and since predictability does not stop me doing this, neither does it stop me asking the question of principle, 'What *ought* one to do in a case like this?'

So the essential part of moral thought, that which consists in trying to form for oneself and others principles of conduct, is not made futile by any advance in our powers of prediction that could possibly take place. The ability to predict and explain will not curtail the freedom which engenders moral thought, though it will, by increasing our knowledge and power, greatly increase both the potential effectiveness and the burdensomeness of that thought. It may also make us more charitable; but charity and the making of moral judgements are not incompatible.

5 · BACKSLIDING

5.1. THE ethical theory which has been briefly set out in the preceding chapters is a type of prescriptivism, in that it maintains that it is one of the characteristics of moral terms, and one which is a sufficiently essential characteristic for us to call it part of the meaning of these terms, that judgements containing them are, as typically used, intended as guides to conduct. Now there is one objection to all kinds of prescriptivism which is so commonly made, and is of such intrinsic interest, that it requires a chapter to itself. This is the objection that, if moral judgements were prescriptive, then it would be impossible to accept some moral judgement and yet act contrary to it. But, it is maintained (in Hume's words), ''tis one thing to know virtue, and another to conform the will to it';[1] people are constantly doing what they think they ought not to be doing; therefore prescriptivism must be wrong.

There are two points from the preceding chapter which are relevant to a consideration of this objection. The first is that, there too, we saw that there was a problem for prescriptivists where there ought to be no problem for descriptivists— namely the problem raised by our feeling that 'ought' implies 'can'. We saw that if 'ought' were always, as it is sometimes, purely descriptive, there would be no question of 'ought' implying 'can', and therefore no problem; the problem arises because of the fact that in some, and those the typical and central, of their uses moral judgements have that affinity with imperatives which makes me call both prescriptive. To this extent, the very existence of the problem—the fact that ordinary people feel that 'ought' implies 'can' and that

[1] *Treatise*, iii. 1. i. For a recent development of this objection, see A. C. Ewing, *Second Thoughts in Moral Philosophy*, ch. 1.

this creates philosophical difficulties—is *prima facie* evidence against descriptivism. If a descriptivist were to argue that moral judgements are purely descriptive, and thus do not imply 'can', and that therefore a moralist can happily accept the extremest form of determinism, his argument would not be plausible. Now it must be pointed out that the same sort of manœuvre is possible here: if moral judgements were not prescriptive, there would be no problem about moral weakness; but there is a problem; therefore they are prescriptive. In fact, the argument from moral weakness is very much of a two-edged weapon in the hands of the descriptivist.

The second point to be remembered from the preceding chapter is that, as we saw, not all moral judgements have the full, universally prescriptive force that the perfect specimen has. There are a great many kinds of 'off-colour' moral judgement which do not, like the perfect specimen, 'imply "can"'. Thus the man who says 'I ought but I can't' is not necessarily saying anything absurd; all that he is doing is to use 'ought' in one of the many off-colour ways that are possible. Some of these we listed.

Now we shall see that typical cases of 'moral weakness' are cases where a man *cannot* do what he thinks he ought; but the 'cannot' here requires very careful examination, since in other senses such a man very well can do what he ought. Nevertheless, in discussing moral weakness we have to deal with a special case of 'ought but can't'; and what was said earlier about 'ought but can't' in general will be relevant.

5.2. The view that there is no problem (that is to say no *philosophical* problem) about moral weakness rests in the main on an analogy between the moral words and other common predicates of our language. Since in the case of 'ought' the analogy is not so plausible, let us for a moment take one of the moral *adjectives*, namely 'best'. On the view that we are considering, there is nothing odder about thinking something the best thing to do in the circumstances, but not doing it, than there is about thinking a stone the roundest stone in the vicinity and not picking it up, but picking up some other stone instead. If I am not looking for a round stone, but just for a stone, there will be nothing which requires explanation if I leave the round stone and pick up, say, a jagged one; and if I am not seeking to do the best thing in the circumstances, but just wondering what to do, there will be nothing that requires explanation if I choose to do what I think to be, say, the worst possible thing to do and leave undone what I think the best thing to do.

One will be likely, that is to say, to think that there is no problem (given that one has considered the matter at all), if one assimilates moral predicates to ordinary descriptive predicates, and ignores their differences. To think that there is no problem is, as we have seen, the mark of a descriptivist. This is a matter of degree. Only the most out-and-out descriptivist will be completely unworried by the possibility of there being a problem; most descriptivists are prepared to admit that if someone does what he says is the worst possible thing to do, an explanation is called for. But nevertheless the attitude of a moral philosopher to this question puts him, as I have already implied, on one side or the other of one of the deepest cleavages in ethics—that between descriptivists and prescriptivists.

For a certain kind of descriptivist, indeed, the existence of 'moral weakness' will still present a problem—namely any descriptivist who approaches these questions in a way which goes back to Aristotle and beyond, but has been associated especially (how justly, I do not know) with the name of Aquinas. This is to say that there is a 'law of nature' (a true but synthetic universal proposition) that all things do, as a matter of fact, seek the good and eschew the evil. The logical properties of this proposition would be like those of the proposition that silkmoths lay their eggs in mulberry-trees—except that the latter is more restricted in scope. Only silkmoths seek mulberry-trees to lay their eggs in, but *everything* seeks the good. Naturally it will not do to say that everything just *happens* to seek the good; this must therefore be some sort of synthetic necessary truth—but perhaps the same would be said about the proposition that silkmoths lay their eggs in mulberry-trees—they do not just happen to lay their eggs there; they do it because that is their *nature*. The concept of 'natural necessity' that is here said to be involved is exceedingly obscure and elusive. I find it much more credible to say that the only kind of necessity here is a logical necessity; in so far as, and in the sense that, it is true at all that everything seeks the good, it is true in virtue of the meanings of 'good' and 'seek'. And this should teach us something about the meaning of the word 'good', and of other such words—namely that they are not purely descriptive. In any case, since this kind of descriptivist will have the same problem on his hands as the prescriptivist, no separate treatment is perhaps necessary.

5.3. Nevertheless it is incumbent on the prescriptivist to say why there is a problem, and to do something about elucidating it. The problem is posed by the fact that moral judgements, in their central use, have it as their function to guide conduct. If this is their function, how can we think, for example, that we ought not to be doing a certain thing (i.e. accept the view that we ought not to be doing it as a guide to our conduct) and then not be guided by it? No one can say that there is no problem here, unless he denies that it is the function of moral judgements to guide conduct.

There are analogies here between expressions like 'think good' and 'think that I ought', on the one hand, and the word 'want' on the other. These analogies are what give force to the old maxim referred to in the previous section, that everything seeks the good. For the Greek and Latin words for 'to seek' (*ephiesthai*, *appetere*) mean also 'to want'. It has rightly been said that 'the primitive sign of wanting is trying to get';[1] and this should warn us that to want something, and espe-

[1] G. E. M. Anscombe, *Intention*, p. 67.

cially to want something more than anything else (where this is the genuine active kind of want and not mere 'idle wishing') is to have a very different kind of thing going on in our minds from what we have when we think that some descriptive proposition is true (for example that a certain cloud is shaped like a duck). To speak very crudely, the kind of thought that we have when we want something belongs with the kinds of thought that are expressed in prescriptive language, such as choices, resolves, requests, prayers, and, lastly, moral and other evaluative judgements. To draw attention to the close logical relations, on the one hand between wanting and thinking good, and on the other between wanting and doing something about getting what one wants, is to play into the hands of the prescriptivist; for it is to provide yet another link between thinking good and action.

5.4. We must not, however, become so obsessed by the analogies between wanting and making value-judgements that we ignore their differences. Doing just this, perhaps, led Socrates into his famous troubles over the question of moral weakness.[1] It is in their universalizability that value-judgements differ from desires (9.1); and nearly all the difficulties of Socrates stem from failing to notice this. In this respect wanting is like assenting to a singular imperative, not to a moral or other value-judgement. If I am trying to make up my mind what to do, I may simply ask myself what I most want to do; or I may ask myself what I ought to do. If I want to do A in these circumstances, I am not committed to wanting anyone else placed in exactly or relevantly similar circumstances to do likewise. But if I think that I ought to do A in these circumstances, I am committed to thinking that anyone else similarly placed ought to do the same. This means that making up my mind what I ought to do is a much more difficult and complex matter than making up my mind what I want to do; and it is these complexities that lead to the

[1] See, e.g., Aristotle, *Nicomachean Ethics*, 1145^{b}25.

problem of moral weakness, and their unravelling to its solution. In making up my mind what I most want to do I have to consult only my own desires. But in making up my mind what I ought to do I have to consider more than this; I have to ask myself 'What maxim (to use Kant's term) can I accept as of *universal* application in cases like this, whether or not *I* play the part in the situation which I am playing now?'

Are we not all, frequently, in circumstances in which we should most like to do *A*, but should very much dislike it if someone did *A* in similar circumstances when we were the victims of his act? I mention this case as an example only, not meaning to imply that all cases of moral weakness are cases where it leads us to harm other people's interests. Indeed, moral weakness is most typically exhibited in falling short of our *ideals*, which need not, as I shall later show, have anything to do with other people's interests (8.4 f.). But in all cases moral weakness is the tendency not to do ourselves something which *in general* we commend, or to do something which *in general* we condemn. This is perhaps the central difficulty of the moral life; and it is no accident that this moral difficulty is reflected in a similarly central difficulty in theoretical ethics. Some moral philosophers speak as if it were easy to make up one's mind what one ought to do. It would indeed be easy, if either of two one-sided ethical theories were a full account of the matter. If deciding what we ought to do were a mere matter of our own desires—like deciding what we most want to do—then it would be a relatively easy task. We should decide what we most wanted to do, and, if it were in our power, do it. To put the same point in a more technical way: if moral judgements were *singular* prescriptives of some sort, then there would be less difficulty in deciding which of them to accept, and acceptance of them would lead to action; there could be no question of weakness of will. That was why Socrates, who paid insufficient attention to the universalizability of moral judgements, found himself saying that there was no such thing as weakness of will.

5.5. That is one spurious way of easing our moral difficulties. The other way consists in accepting the universalizability of moral judgements, and the descriptive meaning that goes with it, and forgetting the universal *prescriptiveness* of moral principles. Then it again becomes easier to make up one's mind what one ought to do, because one is no longer, in saying that one ought to do *A*, prescribing to oneself. If this view were correct, I could decide that I, and that anyone in like circumstances, ought to do *A*, and then, without any hint of going back on what I had decided, not do *A*. There are a great many things which we should be perfectly prepared to say that we ought to do if we did not think that, in saying this, we were committing ourselves to any prescription, and thus action. The real difficulty of making a moral decision is, as I have said before, that of finding some action to which one is prepared to commit oneself, and which at the same time one is prepared to accept as exemplifying a principle of action binding on anyone in like circumstances. This is what makes the moral life, for one who takes it seriously, so appallingly difficult.

So difficult is it, in fact—so great is the strain between prescriptivity and universalizability in certain situations—that something has to give; and this is the explanation of the phenomenon of moral weakness. Not only do *we* give, because we are morally weak; we have found for ourselves a language which shares our weakness, and gives just where we do. For moral language is a human institution. It is the business of the moral philosopher to say, not what the logical behaviour of moral terms *would* be like, if they were devised by and for the use of angels, but what it actually is like.[1] To use another of Kant's expressions, a 'holy' moral language would be a very simple one; it would consist of universalizable prescriptive

[1] Cf. Ewing, op. cit., p. 13.

judgements without any way of escaping from either their prescriptivity or their universality. It would, in fact, be like the evaluative language described in the last chapter of *The Language of Morals* (which was, it will be remembered, a simplified artificial model) without any of the escape-routes for backsliders which are so amply provided in our actual moral language, and which were, some of them, described in the body of the book (e.g. *LM* 7.5, 9.4, 11.2). No shift of ground from the viewpoint of that book is implied in saying that human moral language, unlike a holy or angelic moral language, has, built into its logic, all manner of ways of evading the rigour of pure prescriptive universality. These we shall have to chart in more detail. But nevertheless it would be a slander upon human moral language and on its users to claim that they do not even *aspire* to have universal prescriptive principles; not all who speak morally have already given up the struggle in one of the two ways just referred to, by reconciling themselves to a moral language that is either not prescriptive or not fully universal.

An angel, in making up his mind about a moral question concerning his own conduct, might proceed as follows. He might ask himself to what action he was prepared to commit himself, and at the same time prepared to accept as exemplifying a principle of action binding on anyone in like circumstances. As we have seen, this question is an appallingly difficult one in many situations—the source of the difficulty, we might say, is that in setting out to live morally we are aspiring to be like angels, which is a formidable undertaking. But angels, unlike human beings, do not find any difficulty in answering such questions, because, having holy wills and no selfish inclinations, they do not ever want to do actions whose maxims they cannot universalize. But we are not angels; and therefore, although the *simplest* logic for a moral language would be that of the universalizable prescriptive, we shy at this rigorous and austere simplicity, and, in our vain struggles to find a more comfortable way of speaking, have introduced complexities into the logic of our moral language—vain struggles, because the ideal of pure universal prescriptive moral principles obstinately remains with us, and we are not in the end satisfied with anything which falls short of it.

The complexities are very great, and it will be impossible to mention all of them.[1] The inquiry into them will be, as are most philosophical inquiries, at one and the same time about language and about what happens; for to ask about different senses of 'ought' and of 'think that one ought', in the way that the philosopher asks this, is at the same time to ask about different possible states of mind; the two inquiries are inseparable. One cannot study language, in a philosophical way, without studying the world that we are talking about.[2]

5.6. Here, however, it is necessary to qualify somewhat the expression 'different senses of "ought" '. The impression may have been given by certain passages in *The Language of Morals* that moral words are somehow ambiguous, in that they have a series of distinct senses, so that one could ask a man in which sense he was using them—for example the 'inverted commas', the 'ironic', the 'conventional', and so on (*LM* 7.5). It is wrong to say this. Fortunately Professor Nowell-Smith has now provided us with a terminology for saying much better what I was trying to say. He has invented the expression 'Janus-word' to describe words of the sort we are considering, which have two or more aspects to their meaning, one of which may on occasion be emphasized to the neglect of the others.[3] We cannot say that such a word is ambiguous; it is indeed an inseparable element in its meaning that it can shift in this way. The human word 'ought', unlike its counterpart in an angelic moral language, not only faces both ways in the

[1] For a somewhat more detailed account, with which I largely agree, see Mr. P. L. Gardiner's very helpful article 'On assenting to a moral principle', *Aristotelian Society*, lv (1954/5), 23.

[2] See Austin, *Philosophical Papers*, p. 130 (also in *Aristotelian Society*, lvii (1956/7), 8).   [3] See P. H. Nowell-Smith, *Ethics*, Index s.v.

sense of having both descriptive and prescriptive meaning—for the angelic word does that—but can sometimes look in the direction that suits its user's interests, and bury its other face in the sand. Even if we are at our most moral when we say that we ought to be doing such and such a thing (getting up, for example), and fully intend to set about doing it there and then, we know only too well that if our moral strength were to fail us at the last moment, and we did not get up, we could still go on saying that we thought that we ought to be getting up—and saying it, though in a way in an attenuated sense, without in another way departing from the meaning of the word as we were using it all along; for all along the meaning of the word was such that we *could* backslide in this way.

There are many different methods of backsliding without appearing to. The commonest, perhaps, of these subterfuges is that known as special pleading. We start off as if we were prepared to accept a certain moral principle as binding on everybody; and we start off by accepting it as prescriptive, and therefore as committing *us* in particular to acting in accordance with the principle. But when we consider how contrary to our own interests it is for us to act in accordance with the principle, we weaken. While continuing to prescribe that everyone *else* (or at any rate everyone whose interests do not especially concern us) should act in accordance with the principle, we do not so prescribe to ourselves (for to do this fully and in earnest would commit us to acting). The word 'ought' can remain universal in that it retains all the descriptive meaning that it ever had; but it ceases to express a universal prescription—the prescription is not universal and the universality is only descriptive. To restore the appearance of prescriptive universality, we substitute, in our own case, for genuine prescriptiveness, a mere *feeling*, varying in strength, that we are not playing our part in the scheme which we claim to be accepting (that we are, as it were, leading our regiment from behind). This feeling is called a guilty conscience. It is essential to the success of this manœuvre that the feeling should not, at the time, be too strong. The man who wishes to act against his conscience must make sure that his conscience is less powerful than the desires which oppose it; for if conscience pricks us too hard it will prick us into doing the action, and genuine prescriptive universality will be restored.

Suppose, however, that this does not happen, and that we fail to do the required action, and merely feel uncomfortable about it. Has the expression 'think that I ought' changed its meaning for us? We have, indeed, accepted, as exemplifying the state of mind called 'thinking that I ought', something less robust than formerly; but then from the start the expression 'think that I ought' had the potentiality of such a decline—it is an expression of human language, and humans are always doing this sort of thing. There are, indeed, many ways in which it can lose its robustness without, in a sense, departing from its original meaning; we shall notice some others later.

5.7. I have been speaking as if we were extremely self-conscious and purposive about adopting such a device as I have described. Now there are indeed people who know what they are going about when they do this; such are the real hypocrites. But this is not the state of most of us. Far from it being a matter of freely chosen policy to think in this way, most of us find it impossibly hard, not being angels, to think in any other. Our morality is formed of principles and ideals which we do not succeed in persuading ourselves to fulfil. And this *inability* to realize our ideals is well reflected in the highly significant names given in both Greek and English to this condition: Greek calls it *akrasia*—literally 'not being strong enough (sc. to control oneself)'; and English calls it 'moral weakness' or 'weakness of will'. Nor is this the only evidence that the state of mind that most people are thinking of when they speak of weakness of will involves an inability, in some sense, to do what we think we ought. There are two

extremely well-worn passages in literature which are constantly quoted in this controversy, usually against the prescriptivist position. Since those who quote them frequently
show themselves unaware of the contexts in which they occur,
I shall quote them at length, in order to show how many
references there are to the powerlessness of the speakers. The
first describes Medea, trying to resist the onset of love for
Jason:

> Meanwhile, Aeetes' daughter's heart took fire;
> Her struggling Reason could not quell Desire.
> 'This madness how can I resist?', she cried;
> 'No use to fight; some God is on its side . . .
> Dash from your maiden breast these flames it feels!
> Ah, if I could, the less would be my ills.
> Alas I cannot quench them; an unknown
> Compulsion bears me, all reluctant, down.
> Urged this way—that—on Love's or Reason's course,
> I see and praise the better: do the worse.'[1]

Ovid here again and again stresses the helplessness of
Medea; and so does St. Paul stress his own helplessness in
the famous passage from Romans vii:

We know that the law is spiritual; but I am not: I am unspiritual, the purchased slave of sin. I do not even acknowledge
my own actions as mine, for what I do is not what I want to do,
but what I detest. But if what I do is against my will, it means that
I agree with the law and hold it to be admirable. But as things are,
it is no longer I who perform the action, but sin that lodges in me.
For I know that nothing good lodges in me—in my unspiritual
nature, I mean—for though the will to do good is there, the deed
is not. The good which I want to do, I fail to do; but what I do is
the wrong which is against my will; and if what I do is against my
will, clearly it is no longer I who am the agent, but sin that has its
lodging in me. I discover this principle, then: that when I want to
do the right, only the wrong is within my reach. In my inmost self
I delight in the law of God, but I perceive that there is in my

[1] Ovid, *Metamorphoses*, vii. 20.

bodily members a different law, fighting against the law that my
reason approves and making me a prisoner under the law that is in
my members, the law of sin. Miserable creature that I am, who is
there to rescue me out of this body doomed to death? God alone,
through Jesus Christ our Lord! Thanks be to God! In a word
then, I myself, subject to God's law as a rational being, am yet, in
my unspiritual nature, a slave to the law of sin.[1]

The impression given by these two passages is very different from that conveyed by descriptivist philosophers who
quote scraps from them out of context. Taken as a whole,
these passages do not even run counter to the summary view
which I put forward in *The Language of Morals*. For I said
there that I proposed to use the word 'value-judgement' in
such a way that 'the test, whether someone is using the judgement "I ought to do X" as a value-judgement or not, is "Does
he or does he not recognize that if he assents to the judgement, he must also assent to the command "Let me do X"?'
And earlier I said 'It is a tautology to say that we cannot sincerely assent to a command addressed to ourselves, and *at the
same time* not perform it, if now is the occasion for performing
it, and it is in our (physical and psychological) power to do
so'.[2] The purpose of putting in the words 'physical and
psychological power' was precisely to meet the possible objection which we are considering. Nobody in his senses would
maintain that a person who assents to an imperative must
(analytically) act on it even when he is unable to do so. But
this is what I should have to have been maintaining, if these
quotations from Ovid and St. Paul were to serve as counter-
examples to my view. It is not in Medea's or St. Paul's psychological power to act on the imperatives that are entailed by
the moral judgements which they are making.

[1] Tr. from the *New English Bible*. The new translators, by writing 'The
good which I want to do, I fail to do' (the Greek has merely 'I do not do'),
show that they agree with my interpretation of the passage.
[2] *LM* 11.2 (p. 168) and 2.2 (p. 20). For the use of 'command' see
LM 1.2.

5.8. We see, therefore, that the typical case of moral weakness, as opposed to that of hypocrisy, is a case of 'ought but can't'. We have therefore to put it in its place within the general account of 'ought but can't' given above (4.1). What is it that distinguishes 'psychological' impossibility from 'physical', and this kind of 'psychological' impossibility from others? And what happens to 'ought' in all these cases? We saw that 'physical' impossibility (and also such allied cases as impossibility due to lack of knowledge or skill) causes an imperative to be withdrawn altogether, as inconsistent with the admission of impossibility; but that in a similar case an 'ought' does not have to be withdrawn but only down-graded. It no longer carries prescriptive force in the particular case, though it may continue to do so with regard to actions in similar circumstances (similar, except that the action is possible). I referred to this phenomenon as 'a lifting of a corner of the net'. We are now, perhaps, in a better position to understand it. We also saw that, although the prescription for the particular case has to be withdrawn, this does not prevent agony of mind, or even, in some cases, social reprobation. Jocasta was the victim of destiny, and knew it; but she hanged herself, and people no doubt called her incestuous, which is a term of disapproval.

In cases of moral weakness, where the impossibility is psychological, remorse and disapproval are even more in place; for, though unable to overcome this temptation, they keep alive the will-power which may overcome lesser ones. It is therefore not a consequence of our account of the matter, which stresses the impossibility of resisting the temptation, that the morally weak man is exempt from adverse moral judgements. In terms of the preceding chapter, the question 'What shall I do?' arises for him (as it does not in cases of physical impossibility); and even if we can be sure that he will answer it in a certain way, it may nevertheless be of value to say that he ought not to act so, in order to reassert the general prescriptive principle. St. Paul gives plenty of evidence of remorse, and Medea was no doubt subject to parental dis-approval. St. Paul, we may be sure, did not want himself to sin likewise on future occasions; and Aeetes did not want his other daughters to go falling for foreign adventurers. To this extent their remarks were prescriptive. But it was clearly of no immediate use for either St. Paul or Medea or Aeetes to prescribe for the particular cases. Sometimes, by uttering a prescription, another person may help a morally weak agent to overcome his moral weakness—the actual utterance, by rein-forcing the will of the agent, alters the situation, so that what was impossible becomes possible. But the cases we have been considering may be supposed to lie beyond the reach of such help on the part of fellow humans—though the divine help which St. Paul invokes is partly of this kind.

The form of prescription is preserved, however (and this shows how reluctant we are to suppress it) in the curious metaphor of divided personality which, ever since this subject was first discussed, has seemed so natural. One part of the personality is made to issue commands to the other, and to be angry or grieved when they are disobeyed; but the other part is said either to be unable to obey, or to be so depraved as not to want to, and to be stronger than the part which commands. Medea actually uses the imperative; and St. Paul speaks of a 'law' which he 'agrees with' or 'consents unto' (*Rev. Version*). And so two interpretations of this phenomenon become pos-sible, both of them metaphorical, and both consistent with prescriptivism. The first is that the person who accepts some moral judgement but does not act on it is actually giving commands to himself, but unable to obey them because of a recalcitrant lower nature or 'flesh'; the other is that he is, in his whole personality or real self, ceasing to prescribe to him-self (though there may be a part of him that goes on prescrib-ing, and though he may be quite ready to prescribe to others). These two metaphors are so natural and so deeply imprinted in our common speech that the philosopher who wishes to abandon them in pursuit of literalness will have to invent his own language. Cases differ, and possibly one metaphor is sometimes more appropriate and sometimes another.

5.9. We may conclude, at any rate, that typical cases of moral weakness do not constitute a counter-example to prescriptivism, as I have been maintaining it. But, since it may be objected that there are other cases which do provide counter-examples, it will be helpful to approach the problem from the other end, and ask what sort of case would provide a counter-example to prescriptivism, and whether it exists.

As we have seen, it will not do to quote cases in which people *cannot* bring themselves to do what they think they ought to do. The fact that in such cases it is often true that a man is *physically* in a position, and strong, knowledgeable, and skilful enough, &c., to do what he thinks he ought, is irrelevant. For, whether or not the psychological inability down-grades the 'ought', as I have suggested, it certainly makes it impossible to act on any prescription that may survive, and so explains how prescriptivity, if it survives, is still compatible with disobedience. We may remark that the fact that 'physical' possibility may be unimpaired is the cause of a common initial reluctance to accept the account of the matter which I have given. It cannot be said, it is objected, that the morally weak person *cannot* do what he thinks he ought, because he is obviously as able as the rest of us. But 'able' here refers only to 'physical' ability. In a deeper sense the man cannot do the act. This is clearest in cases of compulsive neuroses in which 'psychological' impossibility comes close to 'physical'; but it holds also in more normal cases of weakness of will, as the very word 'weakness' indicates.

Nor will it do to quote cases in which a man goes on saying that he ought, but fails to act, even though he can act, in every sense of 'can'. For this is the case of what I called purposive backsliding, or hypocrisy; and these are allowed for. If a man does what he says he ought not to, though perfectly able to

resist the temptation to do it, then there is something wrong
with what he says, as well as with what he does. In the simplest case it is insincerity; he is not saying what he really
thinks. In other cases it is self-deception; he thinks that he
thinks he ought, but he has escaped his own notice using
'ought' in an off-colour way. The residual feelings of guilt
have supplied the place of real prescriptiveness. There are
endless possible variations upon this theme; but until one is
produced which really does run counter to prescriptivism, the
prescriptivist need not be concerned.

Equally irrelevant is the case of the man who *thought* that
he ought to do something, but, now that the time has come
to do it, has let pass from his mind either the thought that he
ought, or the thought that now is the time. And so is that of
the man who thinks that in general *one ought*, but has not got
as far as realizing that *his* present case falls under this principle. These cases can be ruled out by confining our attention
to cases in which a man does not do what he thinks (now) that
he ought *to be* doing.[1]

Then there are the cases of people who *think* that they
ought, but lack complete moral conviction. They may be
using the word 'ought' in the most full-blooded possible way;
but they are not so *sure* that they ought, as to commit themselves to action. These cases, likewise, present no difficulty.

Then there is the case, mentioned already above and in *LM*
11.2, in which a man, in saying that he ought, means no more
than that the action in question is required by the accepted
morality of his society, or that it is the sort of action, the
thought of whose omission induces in him certain feelings.
Since such a man is not using the word 'ought' prescriptively,
and since I have allowed for such uses, this case needs no
further discussion.

In all this, we find no case that provides a true counter-
example. And since I myself am unable even to describe such

[1] I owe this useful way of putting the matter to Gardiner, op. cit., p. 31.

a case, let alone to find one in real life, I am content to leave the search to critics of prescriptivism.

Lastly, it may be objected that I have been altogether too elusive—a common fault in philosophy at the present time. In *The Language of Morals* I performed what some have thought an evasive manœuvre by *defining* 'value-judgement' in such a way that if a man did not do what he thought he ought, he could not be using the word evaluatively. I have in this book done something similar with the word 'prescriptive' —only with the qualifications made above. The purpose of both manœuvres was, however, not to evade objections but to clarify the problem by locating it where it can be seen. The problem exists for evaluative or prescriptive uses of moral words; and it is therefore necessary to know which these are. Therefore we have to exclude from the category 'evaluative' or 'universally prescriptive' such uses as do not belong to it. This I tried to do in *The Language of Morals*, and have tried to do in greater detail in this chapter. This is clarification only. The substantive part of the prescriptivist thesis is *that there are* prescriptive uses of these words, and that these uses are important and central to the words' meaning. That they are important and central is shown by the fact that the problems which notoriously arise concerning moral language would not arise unless there were these uses. Such problems are: the impossibility of defining moral words naturalistically (*LM* 11.3); the problems raised by ' "ought" implies "can" ' (4.1 ff.); the problem discussed in this chapter; and others besides. All these problems are indications that moral language is stronger meat than the bellies of descriptivists are accustomed to.

But that prescriptive uses of moral language *exist*, at any rate, cannot be doubted. Prescriptivism would be refuted if it could be shown that we do not ever use moral words in the way that I have characterized as prescriptive. To counter this attack, it is only necessary to produce examples of such a use, and to ask the reader whether he finds them at all untypical.

I will produce just one. If a man is faced with a difficult moral choice, and asks a friend or adviser 'What do you think I ought to do?', is it not sometimes the case that if he says 'You ought to do A', and if the man then proceeds not to do A, he will be said to have rejected the advice?

PART II
MORAL REASONING

And as ye would that men should do to you, do ye also to them likewise.
ST. LUKE, VI, 31

6 · A MORAL ARGUMENT

6.1. HISTORICALLY, one of the chief incentives to the study of ethics has been the hope that its findings might be of help to those faced with difficult moral problems. That this is still a principal incentive for many people is shown by the fact that modern philosophers are often reproached for failing to make ethics relevant to morals.[1] This is because one of the main tenets of many recent moral philosophers has been that the most popular method by which it was sought to bring ethics to bear on moral problems was not feasible—namely the method followed by the group of theories loosely known as 'naturalist'.

The method of naturalism is so to characterize the *meanings* of the key moral terms that, given certain factual premisses, not themselves moral judgements, moral conclusions can be deduced from them. If this could be done, it was thought that it would be of great assistance to us in making moral decisions; we should only have to find out the non-moral facts, and the moral conclusion as to what we ought to do would follow. Those who say that it cannot be done leave themselves the task of giving an alternative account of moral reasoning.

Naturalism seeks to make the findings of ethics *relevant* to

---

[1] I have tried to fill in some of the historical background of these reproaches, and to assess the justification for them, in my article in *The Philosophy of C. D. Broad*, ed. P. Schilpp.

moral decisions by making the former not morally *neutral*. It is a very natural assumption that if a statement of ethics is relevant to morals, then it cannot be neutral as between different moral judgements; and naturalism is a tempting view for those who make this assumption. Naturalistic definitions are not morally neutral, because with their aid we could show that statements of non-moral facts *entailed* moral conclusions. And some have thought that unless such an entailment can be shown to hold, the moral philosopher has not made moral reasoning possible.

One way of escaping this conclusion is to say that the relation linking a set of non-moral premises with a moral conclusion is not one of entailment, but that some other logical relation, peculiar to morals, justifies the inference. This is the view put forward, for example, by Mr. Toulmin.[1] Since I have argued elsewhere against this approach, I shall not discuss it here. Its advocates have, however, hit upon an important insight: that moral reasoning does not necessarily proceed by way of *deduction* of moral conclusions from non-moral premises. Their further suggestion, that therefore it makes this transition by means of some other, peculiar, non-deductive kind of inference, is not the only possibility. It may be that moral reasoning is not, typically, any kind of 'straight-line' or 'linear' reasoning from premises to conclusion.

6.2. A parallel from the philosophy of science will perhaps make this point clear. It is natural to suppose that what the scientist does is to reason from premises, which are the data of observation, to conclusions, which are his 'scientific laws', by means of a special sort of inference called 'inductive'. Against this view, Professor Popper has forcibly argued that in science there are no inferences other than deductive; the typical procedure of scientists is to propound hypotheses, and then look for ways of testing them—i.e. experiments which,

---

[1] S. E. Toulmin, *The Place of Reason in Ethics*, esp. pp. 38–60. See my review in *Philosophical Quarterly*, i (1950/1), 372, and *LM* 3.4.

if they are false, will show them to be so. A hypothesis which, try as we may, we fail to falsify, we accept provisionally, though ready to abandon it if, after all, further experiment refutes it; and of those that are so accepted we rate highest the ones which say most, and which would, therefore, be most likely to have been falsified if they were false. The only inferences which occur in this process are deductive ones, from the truth of certain observations to the falsity of a hypothesis. There is no reasoning which proceeds from the data of observation to the *truth* of a hypothesis. Scientific inquiry is rather a kind of *exploration*, or looking for hypotheses which will stand up to the test of experiment.[1]

We must ask whether moral reasoning exhibits any similar features. I want to suggest that it too is a kind of exploration, and not a kind of linear inference, and that the only inferences which take place in it are deductive. What we are doing in moral reasoning is to look for moral judgements and moral principles which, when we have considered their logical consequences and the facts of the case, we can still accept. As we shall see, this approach to the problem enables us to reject the assumption, which seemed so natural, that ethics cannot be relevant to moral decisions without ceasing to be neutral. This is because we are not going to demand any inferences in our reasoning other than deductive ones, and because none of these deductive inferences rely for their validity upon naturalistic definitions of moral terms.

Two further parallels may help to make clear the sense in which ethics is morally neutral. In the kind of scientific reasoning just described, mathematics plays a major part, for many of the deductive inferences that occur are mathematical in character. So we are bound to admit that mathematics is relevant to scientific inquiry. Nevertheless, it is also neutral,

---

[1] K. R. Popper, *The Logic of Scientific Discovery* (esp. pp. 32 f.). See also his article in C. A. Mace (ed.), *British Philosophy in the Mid-Century*, p. 155.

in the sense that no discoveries about matters of physical fact can be made with the aid of mathematics alone, and that no mathematical inference can have a conclusion which says more, in the way of prediction of observations, than its premisses implicitly do.

An even simpler parallel is provided by the rules of games. The rules of a game are neutral as between the players, in the sense that they do not, by themselves, determine which player is going to win. In order to decide who wins, the players have to play the game in accordance with the rules, which involves their making, themselves, a great many individual decisions. On the other hand, the 'neutrality' of the rules of a game does not turn it into a game of chance, in which the bad player is as likely to win as the good.

Ethical theory, which determines the meanings and functions of the moral words, and thus the 'rules' of the moral 'game', provides only a clarification of the conceptual framework within which moral reasoning takes place; it is therefore, in the required sense, neutral as between different moral opinions. But it is highly relevant to moral reasoning because, as with the rules of a game, there could be no such thing as moral reasoning without this framework, and the framework dictates the form of the reasoning. It follows that naturalism is not the only way of providing for the possibility of moral reasoning; and this may, perhaps, induce those who have espoused naturalism as a way of making moral thought a rational activity to consider other possibilities.

The rules of moral reasoning are, basically, two, corresponding to the two features of moral judgements which I argued for in the first half of this book, prescriptivity and universalizability. When we are trying, in a concrete case, to decide what we ought to do, what we are looking for (as I have already said) is an action to which we can commit ourselves (prescriptivity) but which we are at the same time prepared to accept as exemplifying a principle of action to be prescribed for others in like circumstances (universalizability). If, when we consider some proposed action, we find that, when universalized, it yields prescriptions which we cannot accept, we reject this action as a solution to our moral problem—if we cannot universalize the prescription, it cannot become an 'ought'.

It is to be noticed that, troublesome as was the problem of moral weakness when we were dealing theoretically with the logical character of the moral concepts, it cannot trouble us here. For if a person is going to reason seriously at all about a moral question, he has to presuppose that the moral concepts are going, in his reasoning, to be used prescriptively. One cannot start a moral argument about a certain proposal on the basis that, whatever the conclusion of it, it makes no difference to what anybody is to do. When one has arrived at a conclusion, one may then be too weak to put it into practice. But *in arguing* one has to discount this possibility; for, as we shall see, to abandon the prescriptivity of one's moral judgements is to unscrew an essential part of the logical mechanism on which such arguments rely. This is why, if a person were to say 'Let's have an argument about this grave moral question which faces us, but let's not think of any conclusion we may come to as requiring anybody to *do* one thing rather than another', we should be likely to accuse him of flippancy, or worse.

6.3. I will now try to exhibit the bare bones of the theory of moral reasoning that I wish to advocate by considering a very simple (indeed over-simplified) example. As we shall see, even this very simple case generates the most baffling complexities; and so we may be pardoned for not attempting anything more difficult to start with.

The example is adapted from a well-known parable.[1] *A* owes money to *B*, and *B* owes money to *C*, and it is the law that creditors may exact their debts by putting their debtors

[1] Matthew xviii. 23.

into prison. *B* asks himself, 'Can I say that I ought to take this measure against *A* in order to make him pay?' He is no doubt *inclined* to do this, or *wants* to do it. Therefore, if there were no question of universalizing his prescriptions, he would assent readily to the *singular* prescription 'Let me put *A* into prison' (4.3). But when he seeks to turn this prescription into a moral judgement, and say, 'I *ought* to put *A* into prison because he will not pay me what he owes', he reflects that this would involve accepting the principle 'Anyone who is in my position ought to put his debtor into prison if he does not pay'. But then he reflects that *C* is in the same position of unpaid creditor with regard to himself (*B*), and that the cases are otherwise identical; and that if anyone in this position ought to put his debtors into prison, then so ought *C* to put him (*B*) into prison. And to accept the moral prescription '*C* ought to put me into prison' would commit him (since, as we have seen, he must be using the word 'ought' prescriptively) to accepting the singular prescription 'Let *C* put me into prison'; and this he is not ready to accept. But if he is not, then neither can he accept the original judgement that he (*B*) ought to put *A* into prison for debt. Notice that the whole of this argument would break down if 'ought' were not being used both universalizably *and prescriptively*; for if it were not being used prescriptively, the step from '*C* ought to put me into prison' to 'Let *C* put me into prison' would not be valid.

The structure and ingredients of this argument must now be examined. We must first notice an analogy between it and the Popperian theory of scientific method. What has happened is that a provisional or suggested moral principle has been rejected because one of its particular consequences proved unacceptable. But an important difference between the two kinds of reasoning must also be noted; it is what we should expect, given that the data of scientific observation are recorded in descriptive statements, whereas we are here dealing with prescriptions. What knocks out a suggested hypothesis,

on Popper's theory, is a singular statement of fact: the hypothesis has the consequence that p; but not-p. Here the logic
is just the same, except that in place of the observation-state-
ments 'p' and 'not-p' we have the singular *prescriptions* 'Let
C put B into prison for debt' and its contradictory. Nevertheless, given that B is disposed to reject the first of these prescriptions, the argument against him is just as cogent as in the
scientific case.

We may carry the parallel further. Just as science, seriously
pursued, is the search for hypotheses and the testing of them
by the attempt to falsify their particular consequences, so
morals, as a serious endeavour, consists in the search for principles and the testing of them against particular cases. Any
rational activity has its discipline, and this is the discipline of
moral thought: to test the moral principles that suggest themselves to us by following out their consequences and seeing
whether we can accept *them*.

No argument, however, starts from nothing. We must
therefore ask what we have to have before moral arguments of
the sort of which I have given a simple example can proceed.
The first requisite is that the facts of the case should be given;
for all moral discussion is about some particular set of facts,
whether actual or supposed. Secondly we have the logical
framework provided by the meaning of the word 'ought' (i.e.
prescriptivity and universalizability, both of which we saw to
be necessary). Because moral judgements have to be universalizable, B cannot say that he ought to put A into prison for
debt without committing himself to the view that C, who is
ex hypothesi in the same position *vis-à-vis* himself, ought to
put *him* into prison; and because moral judgements are prescriptive, this would be, in effect, prescribing to C to put him
into prison; and this he is unwilling to do, since he has a
strong inclination not to go to prison. This inclination gives
us the third necessary ingredient in the argument: if B were
a completely apathetic person, who literally did not mind

what happened to himself or to anybody else, the argument would not touch him. The three necessary ingredients which we have noticed, then, are (1) facts; (2) logic; (3) inclinations. These ingredients enable us, not indeed to arrive at an evaluative conclusion, but to *reject* an evaluative proposition. We shall see later that these are not, in all cases, the only necessary ingredients.

6.4. In the example which we have been using, the position was deliberately made simpler by supposing that B actually stood to some other person in exactly the same relation as A does to him. Such cases are unlikely to arise in practice. But it is not necessary for the force of the argument that B should *in fact* stand in this relation to anyone; it is sufficient that he should consider hypothetically such a case, and see what would be the consequences in it of those moral principles between whose acceptance and rejection he has to decide. Here we have an important point of difference from the parallel scientific argument, in that the crucial case which leads to rejection of the principle can itself be a supposed, not an observed, one. That hypothetical cases will do as well as actual ones is important, since it enables us to guard against a possible misinterpretation of the argument which I have outlined. It might be thought that what moves B is the *fear* that C will actually do to him as he does to A—as happens in the gospel parable. But this fear is not only irrelevant to the moral argument; it does not even provide a particularly strong nonmoral motive unless the circumstances are somewhat exceptional. C may, after all, not find out what B has done to A; or C's moral principles may be different from B's, and independent of them, so that what moral principle B accepts makes no difference to the moral principles on which C acts.

Even, therefore, if C did not exist, it would be no answer to the argument for B to say 'But in my case there is no fear that anybody will ever be in a position to do to me what I am proposing to do to A'. For the argument does not rest on any

such fear. All that is essential to it is that *B* should disregard
the fact that he plays the particular role in the situation which
he does, without disregarding the inclinations which people
have in situations of this sort. In other words, he must be
prepared to give weight to *A*'s inclinations and interests as if
they were his own. This is what turns selfish prudential reasoning into moral reasoning. It is much easier, psychologically,
for *B* to do this if he is actually placed in a situation like *A*'s
vis-à-vis somebody else; but this is not necessary, provided
that he has sufficient imagination to envisage what it is like to
be *A*. For our first example, a case was deliberately chosen in
which little imagination was necessary; but in most normal
cases a certain power of imagination and readiness to use it is
a fourth necessary ingredient in moral arguments, alongside
those already mentioned, viz. logic (in the shape of universalizability and prescriptivity), the facts, and the inclinations
or interests of the people concerned.

It must be pointed out that the absence of even one of
these ingredients may render the rest ineffective. For example,
impartiality by itself is not enough. If, in becoming impartial,
B became also completely dispassionate and apathetic, and
moved as little by other people's interests as by his own, then,
as we have seen, there would be nothing to make him accept
or reject one moral principle rather than another. That is why
those who, like Adam Smith and Professor Kneale, advocate
what have been called 'Ideal Observer Theories' of ethics,
sometimes postulate as their imaginary ideal observer not
merely an impartial spectator, but an impartially *sympathetic*
spectator.[1] To take another example, if the person who faces

[1] It will be plain that there are affinities, though there are also differences, between this type of theory and my own. For such theories see
W. C. Kneale, *Philosophy*, xxv (1950), 162; R. Firth and R. B. Brandt, *Philosophy and Phenomenological Research*, xii (1951/2), 317, and xv (1954/5),
407, 414, 422; and J. Harrison, *Aristotelian Society*, supp. vol. xxviii
(1954), 132. Firth, unlike Kneale, says that the observer must be 'dispassionate', but see Brandt, op. cit., p. 411 n. For a shorter discussion see

the moral decision has no imagination, then even the fact that someone can do the very same thing to him may pass him by. If, again, he lacks the readiness to universalize, then the vivid imagination of the sufferings which he is inflicting on others may only spur him on to intensify them, to increase his own vindictive enjoyment. And if he is ignorant of the material facts (for example about what is likely to happen to a person if one takes out a writ against him), then there is nothing to tie the moral argument to particular choices.

6.5. The best way of testing the argument which we have outlined will be to consider various ways in which somebody in B's position might seek to escape from it. There are indeed a number of such ways; and all of them may be successful, at a price. It is important to understand what the price is in each case. We may classify these manœuvres which are open to B into two kinds. There are first of all the moves which depend on his using the moral words in a different way from that on which the argument relied. We saw that for the success of the argument it was necessary that 'ought' should be used universalizably and prescriptively. If B uses it in a way that is either not prescriptive or not universalizable, then he can escape the force of the argument, at the cost of resigning from the kind of discussion that we thought we were having with him. We shall discuss these two possibilities separately. Secondly, there are moves which can still be made by B, even though he is using the moral words in the same way as we are. We shall examine three different sub-classes of these.

Before dealing with what I shall call the *verbal* manœuvres in detail, it may be helpful to make a general remark. Suppose that we are having a simple mathematical argument with somebody, and he admits, for example, that there are five

Brandt, *Ethical Theory*, p. 173. Since for many Christians God occupies the role of 'ideal observer', the moral judgements which they make may be expected to coincide with those arrived at by the method of reasoning which I am advocating.

eggs in this basket, and six in the other, but maintains that there are a dozen eggs in the two baskets taken together; and suppose that this is because he is using the expression 'a dozen' to mean 'eleven'. It is obvious that we cannot compel him logically to admit that there are not a dozen eggs, in *his* sense of 'dozen'. But it is equally obvious that this should not disturb us. For such a man only appears to be dissenting from us. His dissent is only apparent, because the proposition which his words express is actually consistent with the conclusion which we wish to draw; he *says* 'There are a dozen eggs'; but he *means* what we should express by saying 'There are eleven eggs'; and this we are not disputing. It is important to remember that in the moral case also the dissent may be only apparent, if the words are being used in different ways, and that it is no defect in a method of argument if it does not make it possible to prove a conclusion to a person when he is using words in such a way that the conclusion does not follow.

It must be pointed out, further (since this is a common source of confusion), that in this argument nothing whatever hangs upon our *actual* use of words in common speech, any more than it does in the arithmetical case. That we use the sound 'dozen' to express the meaning that we customarily do use it to express is of no consequence for the argument about the eggs; and the same may be said of the sound 'ought'. There is, however, something which I, at any rate, customarily express by the sound 'ought', whose character is correctly described by saying that it is a universal or universalizable prescription. I hope that what I customarily express by the sound 'ought' is the same as what most people customarily express by it; but if I am mistaken in this assumption, I shall still have given a correct account, so far as I am able, of that which I express by this sound.[1] Nevertheless, this account will interest other people mainly in so far as my

[1] Cf. Moore, *Principia Ethica*, p. 6.

hope that they understand the same thing as I do by 'ought' is fulfilled; and since I am moderately sure that this is indeed the case with many people, I hope that I may be of use to them in elucidating the logical properties of the concept which they thus express.

At this point, however, it is of the utmost importance to stress that the fact that two people express the same thing by 'ought' does not entail that they share the same moral opinions. For the formal, logical properties of the word 'ought' (those which are determined by its *meaning*) are only one of the four factors (listed earlier) whose combination governs a man's moral opinion on a given matter. Thus ethics, the study of the logical properties of the moral words, remains morally neutral (its conclusions neither are substantial moral judgements, nor entail them, even in conjunction with factual premisses); its bearing upon moral questions lies in this, that it makes logically impossible certain combinations of moral and other prescriptions. Two people who are using the word 'ought' in the same way may yet disagree about what ought to be done in a certain situation, either because they differ about the facts, or because one or other of them lacks imagination, or because their different inclinations make one reject some singular prescription which the other can accept. For all that, ethics (i.e. the logic of moral language) is an immensely powerful engine for producing moral agreement; for if two people are willing to use the moral word 'ought', and to use it in the same way (viz. the way that I have been describing), the other possible sources of moral disagreement are all eliminable. People's inclinations about most of the important matters in life tend to be the same (very few people, for example, like being starved or run over by motor-cars); and, even when they are not, there is a way of generalizing the argument, to be described in the next chapter, which enables us to make allowance for differences in inclinations. The facts are often, given sufficient patience, ascertainable. Imagination can be cultivated. If these three factors are looked after, as they can be, agreement on the use of 'ought' is the only other necessary condition for producing moral agreement, at any rate in typical cases. And, if I am not mistaken, this agreement in use is already there in the discourse of anybody with whom we are at all likely to find ourselves arguing; all that is needed is to think clearly, and so make it evident.

After this methodological digression, let us consider what is to be done with the man who professes to be using 'ought' in some different way from that which I have described—because he is not using it prescriptively, or not universalizably. For the reasons that I have given, if he takes either of these courses, he is no longer in substantial moral disagreement with us. Our apparent moral disagreement is really only verbal; for although, as we shall see shortly, there may be a residuum of substantial disagreement, this cannot be moral.[1]

Let us take first the man who is using the word 'ought' prescriptively, but not universalizably. He can say that he ought to put his debtor into prison, although he is not prepared to agree that his creditor ought to put *him* into prison. We, on the other hand, since we are not prepared to admit that our creditors in these circumstances ought to put us into prison, cannot say that we ought to put our debtors into prison. So there is an appearance of substantial moral disagreement, which is intensified by the fact that, since we are both using the word 'ought' prescriptively, our respective views will lead to different particular actions. Different *singular* prescriptions about what to do are (since both our judgements are prescriptive) derivable from what we are respectively saying. But this is not enough to constitute a moral disagreement. For that, we should have to differ, not only about what *is* to be done in some particular case, but about some universal

---

[1] Strictly, we should say 'evaluative'; but for the reason given on p. 90, we can ignore the non-evaluative moral judgements mentioned on pp. 26 f. and in *LM* 11.3

principle concerning what *ought* to be done in cases of a
certain sort; and since *B* is (on the hypothesis considered)
advocating no such universal principle, he is saying nothing
with which we can be in moral or evaluative disagreement.
Considered purely as prescriptions, indeed, our two views
are in substantial disagreement; but the moral, evaluative (i.e.
the *universal* prescriptive) disagreement is only verbal, because,
when the expression of *B*'s view is understood as he means it,
the view turns out not to be a view about the morality of the
action at all. So *B*, by this manœuvre, can go on prescribing
to himself to put *A* into prison, but has to abandon the claim
that he is justifying the action morally, as we understand the
word 'morally'. One may, of course, use any word as one
pleases, at a price. But he can no longer claim to be giving
that sort of justification of his action for which, as I think,
the common expression is 'moral justification' (10.7).

I need not deal at length with the second way in which *B*
might be differing from us in his use of 'ought', viz. by not
using it prescriptively. If he were not using it prescriptively,
it will be remembered, he could assent to the singular prescription 'Let not *C* put me into prison for debt', and yet
assent also to the non-prescriptive moral judgement '*C* ought
to put me into prison for debt'. And so his disinclination to be
put into prison for debt by *C* would furnish no obstacle to his
saying that he (*B*) ought to put *A* into prison for debt. And
thus he could carry out his own inclination to put *A* into
prison with apparent moral justification. The justification
would be, however, only apparent. For if *B* is using the word
'ought' non-prescriptively, then 'I ought to put *A* into prison
for debt' does not entail the singular prescription 'Let me put
A into prison for debt'; the 'moral' judgement becomes quite
irrelevant to the choice of what to do. There would also be
the same lack of substantial moral disagreement as we noticed
in the preceding case. *B* would not be disagreeing with us
other than verbally, so far as the moral question is concerned

(though there might be points of *factual* disagreement between
us, arising from the *descriptive* meaning of our judgements).
The 'moral' disagreement could be only verbal, because
whereas we should be dissenting from the universalizable
prescription '*B* ought to put *A* into prison for debt', *this*
would not be what *B* was expressing, though the words he
would be using would be the same. For *B* would not, by
these words, be expressing a prescription at all.

6.6. So much for the ways (of which my list may well be
incomplete) in which *B* can escape from our argument by
using the word 'ought' in a different way from us. The
remaining ways of escape are open to him even if he is using
'ought' in the same way as we are, viz. to express a universalizable prescription.

We must first consider that class of escape-routes whose
distinguishing feature is that *B*, while using the moral words
in the same way as we are, refuses to make positive moral
judgements at all in certain cases. There are two main variations of this manœuvre. *B* may either say that it is indifferent,
morally, whether he imprisons *A* or not; or he may refuse to
make any moral judgement at all, even one of indifference,
about the case. It will be obvious that if he adopts either of
these moves, he can evade the argument as so far set out. For
that argument only forced him to *reject* the moral judgement
'I ought to imprison *A* for debt'. It did not force him to assent
to any moral judgement; in particular, he remained free to
assent, either to the judgement that he ought not to imprison
A for debt (which is the one that we want him to accept) or to
the judgement that it is neither the case that he ought, nor the
case that he ought not (that is, in short, indifferent); and he
remained free, also, to say 'I am just not making any moral
judgements at all about this case'.

We have not yet, however, exhausted the arguments generated by the demand for universalizability, provided that the
moral words are being used in a way which allows this

demand. For it is evident that these manœuvres could, in principle, be practised in any case whatever in which the morality of an act is in question. And this enables us to place *B* in a dilemma. Either he practises this manœuvre in *every* situation in which he is faced with a moral decision; or else he practises it only *sometimes*. The first alternative, however, has to be sub-divided; for 'every situation' might mean 'every situation in which he himself has to face a moral decision regarding one of his own actions', or it might mean 'every situation in which a moral question arises for him, whether about his own actions or about somebody else's'. So there are three courses that he can adopt: (1) He either refrains altogether from making moral judgements, or makes none except judgements of indifference (that is to say, he either observes a complete moral silence, or says 'Nothing matters morally'; either of these two positions might be called a sort of amoralism); (2) He makes moral judgements in the normal way about other people's actions, but adopts one or other of the kinds of amoralism, just mentioned, with regard to his own; (3) He expresses moral indifference, or will make no moral judgement at all, with regard to *some* of his own actions and those of other people, but makes moral judgements in the normal way about others.

Now it will be obvious that in the first case there is nothing that we can do, and that this should not disturb us. Just as one cannot win a game of chess against an opponent who will not make any moves—and just as one cannot argue mathematically with a person who will not commit himself to any mathematical statements—so moral argument is impossible with a man who will make no moral judgements at all, or—which for practical purposes comes to the same thing—makes only judgements of indifference. Such a person is not entering the arena of moral dispute, and therefore it is impossible to contest with him. He is compelled also—and this is important —to abjure the protection of morality for his own interests.

In the other two cases, however, we have an argument left. If a man is prepared to make positive moral judgements about other people's actions, but not about his own, or if he is prepared to make them about some of his own decisions, but not about others, then we can ask him on what principle he makes the distinction between these various cases. This is a particular application of the demand for universalizability. He will still have left to him the ways of escape from this demand which are available in all its applications, and which we shall consider later. But there is no way of escape which is available in this application, but not in others. He must either produce (or at least admit the existence of) some principle which makes him hold different moral opinions about apparently similar cases, or else admit that the judgements he is making are not moral ones. But in the latter case, he is in the same position, in the present dispute, as the man who will not make any moral judgements at all; he has resigned from the contest.

In the particular example which we have been considering, we supposed that the cases of B and of C, his own creditor, were identical. The demand for universalization therefore compels B to make the same moral judgement, whatever it is, about both cases. He has therefore, unless he is going to give up the claim to be arguing morally, either to say that neither he nor C ought to exercise their legal rights to imprison their debtors; or that both ought (a possibility to which we shall recur in the next section); or that it is indifferent whether they do. But the last alternative leaves it open to B and C to do what they like in the matter; and we may suppose that, though B himself would like to have this freedom, he will be unwilling to allow it to C. It is as unlikely that he will *permit* C to put him (B) into prison as that he will *prescribe* it (10.5). We may say, therefore, that while move (1), described above, constitutes an abandonment of the dispute, moves (2) and (3) really add nothing new to it.

6.7. We must next consider a way of escape which may seem much more respectable than those which I have so far mentioned. Let us suppose that B is a firm believer in the rights of property and the sanctity of contracts. In this case he may say roundly that debtors ought to be imprisoned by their creditors whoever they are, and that, specifically, C ought to imprison him (B), and he (B) ought to imprison A. And he may, unlike the superficially similar person described earlier, be meaning by 'ought' just what we usually mean by it—i.e. he may be using the word prescriptively, realizing that in saying that C ought to put him into prison, he is prescribing that C put him in prison. B, in this case, is perfectly ready to go to prison for his principles, in order that the sanctity of contracts may be enforced. In real life, B would be much more likely to take this line if the situation in which he himself played the role of debtor were not actual but only hypothetical; but this, as we saw earlier, ought not to make any difference to the argument.

We are not yet, however, in a position to deal with this escape-route. All we can do is to say why we cannot now deal with it, and leave this loose end to be picked up later. B, if he is sincere in holding the principle about the sanctity of contracts (or any other universal moral principle which has the same effect in this particular case), may have two sorts of grounds for it. He may hold it on utilitarian grounds, thinking that, unless contracts are rigorously enforced, the results will be so disastrous as to outweigh any benefits that A, or B himself, may get from being let off. This could, in certain circumstances, be a good argument. But we cannot tell whether it is, until we have generalized the type of moral argument which has been set out in this chapter, to cover cases in which the interests of more than two parties are involved. As we saw, it is only the interests of A and B that come into the argument as so far considered (the interests of the third party, C, do not need separate consideration, since C was introduced only in order to show B, if necessary fictionally, a situation in which the roles were reversed; therefore C's interests, being a mere replica of B's, will vanish, as a separate factor, once the A/B situation, and the moral judgements made on it, are universalized). But if utilitarian grounds of the sort suggested are to be adduced, they will bring with them a reference to all the other people whose interests would be harmed by laxity in the enforcement of contracts. This escape-route, therefore, if this is its basis, introduces considerations which cannot be assessed until we have generalized our form of argument to cover 'multilateral' moral situations (7.2 ff.). At present, it can only be said that if B can show that leniency in the enforcement of contracts would really have the results he claims for the community at large, he might be justified in taking the severer course. This will be apparent after we have considered in some detail an example (that of the judge and the criminal) which brings out these considerations even more clearly.

On the other hand, B might have a quite different, non-utilitarian kind of reason for adhering to his principle. He might be moved, not by any weight which he might attach to the interests of other people, but by the thought that to enforce contracts of this sort is necessary in order to conform to some moral or other *ideal* that he has espoused. Such ideals might be of various sorts. He might be moved, for example, by an ideal of abstract justice, of the *fiat justitia, ruat caelum* variety. We have to distinguish such an ideal of justice, which pays no regard to people's interests, from that which is concerned merely to do justice *between* people's interests. It is very important, if considerations of justice are introduced into a moral argument, to know of which sort they are. Justice of the second kind can perhaps be accommodated within a moral view which it is not misleading to call utilitarian (7.4). But this is not true of an ideal of the first kind. It is characteristic of this sort of non-utilitarian ideals that, when they are introduced into moral arguments, they render ineffective the appeal to universalized self-interest which is the foundation of the argument that we have been considering. This is because the person who has whole-heartedly espoused such an ideal (we shall call him the 'fanatic') does not mind if people's interests —even his own—are harmed in the pursuit of it. (8.6, 9.1).

It need not be justice which provides the basis of such an escape-route as we are considering. Any moral ideal would do, provided that it were pursued regardless of other people's interests. For example, B might be a believer in the survival of the fittest, and think that, in order to promote this, he (and everyone else) ought to pursue their own interests by all means in their power and regardless of everyone else's interests. This ideal might lead him, in this particular case, to put A in prison, and he might agree that C ought to do the same to him, if he were not clever enough to avoid this fate. He might think that universal obedience to such a principle would maximize the production of supermen and so make the world a better place. If these were his grounds, it is possible that we might argue with him factually, showing that the universal observance of the principle would not have the results he claimed. But we might be defeated in this factual argument if he had an ideal which made him call the world 'a better place' when the jungle law prevailed; he could then agree to our factual statements, but still maintain that the condition of the world described by us as resulting from the observance of his principle would be better than its present condition. In this case, the argument might take two courses. If we could get him to imagine himself in the position of the weak, who went to the wall in such a state of the world, we might bring him to realize that to hold his principle involved prescribing that things should be done to him, in hypothetical situations, which he could not sincerely prescribe. If so, then the argument would be on the rails again, and could proceed on lines which we have already sketched. But he might stick to his principle and say 'If I were weak, then I ought to go to the wall'. If he did this, he would be putting himself beyond the reach of what we shall call 'golden-rule' or 'utilitarian' arguments by becoming what we shall call a 'fanatic'. Since a great part of the rest of this book will be concerned with people who take this sort of line, it is unnecessary to pursue their case further at this point.

6.8. The remaining manœuvre that B might seek to practise is probably the commonest. It is certainly the one which is most frequently brought up in philosophical controversies on this topic. This consists in a fresh appeal to the facts—i.e. in asserting that there are in fact morally relevant differences between his case and that of others. In the example which we have been considering, we have artificially ruled out this way of escape by assuming that the case of B and C is exactly similar to that of A and B; from this it follows *a fortiori* that there are no morally relevant differences. Since the B/C case may be a hypothetical one, this condition of exact similarity can always be fulfilled, and therefore this manœuvre is based on a misconception of the type of argument against which it is directed. Nevertheless it may be useful, since this objection is so commonly raised, to deal with it at this point, although nothing further will be added thereby to what has been said already.

It may be claimed that no two actual cases would ever be exactly similar; there would always be some differences, and B might allege that some of these were morally relevant. He might allege, for example, that, whereas his family would starve if C put him into prison, this would not be the case if he put A into prison, because A's family would be looked after by A's relatives. If such a difference existed, there might be nothing logically disreputable in calling it morally relevant, and such arguments are in fact often put forward and accepted.

The difficulty, however, lies in drawing the line between those arguments of this sort which are legitimate, and those which are not. Suppose that B alleges that the fact that A has a hooked nose or a black skin entitles him, B, to put him in prison, but that C ought not to do the same thing to him, B, because his nose is straight and his skin white. Is this an argument of equal logical respectability? Can I say that the fact that I have a mole in a particular place on my chin entitles me to further my own interests at others' expense, but that they are forbidden to do this by the fact that they lack this mark of natural pre-eminence?

The answer to this manœuvre is implicit in what has been said already about the relevance, in moral arguments, of hypothetical as well as of actual cases. The fact that no two actual cases are ever identical has no bearing on the problem. For all we have to do is to imagine an identical case in which the roles are reversed. Suppose that my mole disappears, and that my neighbour grows one in the very same spot on his chin. Or, to use our other example, what does B say about a hypothetical case in which he has a black skin or a hooked nose, and A and C are both straight-nosed and white-skinned (9.4; 11.7)? Since this is the same argument, in essentials, as we used at the very beginning, it need not be repeated here. B is in fact faced with a dilemma. Either the property of his own case, which he claims to be morally relevant, is a properly universal property (i.e. one describable without reference to individuals), or it is not. If it is a universal property, then, because of the meaning of the word 'universal', it is a property which might be possessed by another case in which he played a different role (though in fact it may not be); and we can therefore ask him to ignore the fact that it is he himself who plays the role which he does in this case. This will force him to count as morally relevant only those properties which he is prepared to allow to be relevant even when other people have them. And this rules out all the attractive kinds of special pleading. On the other hand, if the property in question is not a properly universal one, then he has not met the demand for universalizability, and cannot claim to be putting forward a moral argument at all.

6.9. It is necessary, in order to avoid misunderstanding, to add two notes to the foregoing discussion. The misunderstanding arises through a too literal interpretation of the common forms of expression—which constantly recur in arguments of this type—'How would you like it if . . . ?' and 'Do as you would be done by'. Though I shall later, for convenience, refer to the type of arguments here discussed as 'golden-rule' arguments, we must not be misled by these forms of expression.

First of all, we shall make the nature of the argument clearer if, when we are asking *B* to imagine himself in the position of his victim, we phrase our question, never in the form 'What *would* you say, or feel, or think, or how *would* you like it, if you were he?', but always in the form 'What *do* you say (*in propria persona*) about a hypothetical case in which you are in your victim's position?' The importance of this way of phrasing the question is that, if the question were put in the first way, *B* might reply 'Well, of course, if anybody did this to me I should resent it very much and make all sorts of adverse moral judgements about the act; but this has absolutely no bearing on the validity of the moral opinion which I am *now* expressing'. To involve him in contradiction, we have to show that he *now* holds an opinion about the hypothetical case which is inconsistent with his opinion about the actual case.

The second thing which has to be noticed is that the argument, as set out, does not involve any sort of deduction of a moral judgement, or even of the negation of a moral judgement, from a factual statement about people's inclinations, interests, &c. We are not saying to *B* 'You are as a matter of fact averse to this being done to you in a hypothetical case; and from this it follows logically that you ought not to do it to another'. Such a deduction would be a breach of Hume's Law ('No "ought" from an "is" '), to which I have repeatedly declared my adherence (*LM* 2.5). The point is, rather, that because of his aversion to its being done to him in the hypothetical case, he cannot accept the singular *prescription* that in the hypothetical case it should be done to him; and this, because of the logic of 'ought', precludes him from accepting the moral judgement that he ought to do likewise to another in the actual case. It is not a question of a factual statement about a person's inclinations being inconsistent with a moral judgement; rather, his inclinations being what they are, he cannot assent sincerely to a certain singular prescription, and if he cannot do this, he cannot assent to a certain universal prescription which entails it, when conjoined with factual statements about the circumstances whose truth he admits. Because of this entailment, if he assented to the factual statements and to the universal prescription, but refused (as he must, his inclinations being what they are) to assent to the singular prescription, he would be guilty of a logical inconsistency.

If it be asked what the relation is between his aversion to being put in prison in the hypothetical case, and his inability to accept the hypothetical singular prescription that if he were in such a situation he should be put into prison, it would seem that the relation is not unlike that between a belief that the cat is on the mat, and an inability to accept the proposition that the cat is not on the mat. Further attention to this parallel will perhaps make the position clearer. Suppose that somebody advances the hypothesis that cats never sit on mats, and that we refute him by pointing to a cat on a mat. The logic of our refutation proceeds in two stages. Of these, the second is: 'Here is a cat sitting on a mat, so it is not the case that cats never sit on mats'. This is a piece of logical deduction; and to it, in the moral case, corresponds the step from 'Let this not be done to me' to 'It is not the case that I ought to do it to another in similar circumstances'. But in both cases there is a first stage whose nature is more obscure, and different in the two cases, though there is an analogy between them.

In the 'cat' case, it is logically possible for a man to look straight at the cat on the mat, and yet believe that there is no cat on the mat. But if a person with normal eyesight and no psychological aberrations does this, we say that he does not understand the meaning of the words, 'The cat is on the mat'. And even if he does not have normal eyesight, or suffers from some psychological aberration (such a phobia of cats, say, that he just *cannot* admit to himself that he is face to face with one), yet, if we can convince him that everyone else can see a cat there, he will have to admit that there *is* a cat there, or be accused of misusing the language.

If, on the other hand, a man says 'But I *want* to be put in prison, if ever I am in that situation', we can, indeed, get as far as accusing him of having eccentric desires; but we cannot, when we have proved to him that nobody else has such a desire, face him with the choice of either saying, with the rest, 'Let this not be done to me', or else being open to the accusation of not understanding what he is saying. For it is not an incorrect use of words to want eccentric things. Logic does not prevent me wanting to be put in a gas chamber if a Jew. It is perhaps true that I logically cannot want for its own sake an experience which I think of as *unpleasant*; for to say that I think of it as unpleasant may be logically inconsistent with saying that I want it for its own sake. If this is so, it is because 'unpleasant' is a prescriptive expression. But 'to be put in prison' and 'to be put in a gas chamber if a Jew', are not prescriptive expressions; and therefore these things can be wanted without offence to logic. It is, indeed, in the logical possibility of wanting *anything* (neutrally described) that the 'freedom' which is alluded to in my title essentially consists. And it is this, as we shall see, that lets by the person whom I shall call the 'fanatic' (9.1 ff.).

There is not, then, a complete analogy between the man who says 'There is no cat on the mat' when there is, and the man who wants things which others do not. But there is a partial analogy, which, having noticed this difference, we may be able to isolate. The analogy is between two relations: the relations between, in both cases, the 'mental state' of these men and what they say. If I believe that there is a cat on the mat I cannot sincerely say that there is not; and, if I want not to be put into prison more than I want anything else, I cannot sincerely say 'Let me be put into prison'. When, therefore, I said above 'His inclinations being what they are, he cannot assent sincerely to a certain singular prescription', I was making an analytic statement (although the 'cannot' is not a logical 'cannot'); for if he were to assent sincerely to the prescription, that would entail *ex vi terminorum* that his inclinations had changed—in the very same way that it is analytically true that, if the other man were to say sincerely that there was a cat on the mat, when before he had sincerely denied this, he must have changed his belief.

If, however, instead of writing 'His inclinations being what they are, he cannot . . .', we leave out the first clause and write simply 'He cannot . . .', the statement is no longer analytic; we are making a statement about his psychology which might be false. For it is logically possible for inclinations to change; hence it is possible for a man to come sincerely to hold an ideal which requires that he himself should be sent to a gas chamber if a Jew. That is the price we have to pay for our freedom. But, as we shall see, in order for reason to have a place in morals it is not necessary for us to close this way of escape by means of a logical barrier; it is sufficient that, men and the world being what they are, we can be very sure that hardly anybody is going to take it with his eyes open. And when we are arguing with one of the vast majority who are not going to take it, the reply that somebody else *might* take it does not help his case against us. In this respect, all moral arguments are *ad hominem*.[1]

---

[1] The above discussion may help to atone for what is confused or even wrong in *LM* 3.3 (p. 42). The remarks there about the possibility or impossibility of accepting certain moral principles gave the impression of creating an impasse; I can, however, plead that in *LM* 4.4 (p. 69) there appeared a hint of the way out which is developed in this book.

7 · UTILITARIANISM

7.1. IT will be obvious that the kind of argument outlined in the preceding chapter, though it offers us the beginning of an idea of how moral arguments might be brought to a conclusion, is far from having reached the point at which a satisfactory theory of moral argument could be founded upon it. In particular, something needs to be said about a difficulty which is of especial interest, not merely in itself, but because it points the way to a further generalization of the method of argument outlined. At the end of the preceding chapter we mentioned the logical possibility of people having different (even eccentric) inclinations. This, as we saw, opens up to those whom I shall call 'fanatics' a way of escape from the argument, at a price. We must now ask whether, for those who are not prepared to pay that price, the method of argument can be generalized to cover cases in which the inclinations of the parties differ.

In the example which we have been discussing, I deliberately took a case where *B* and *A* had the *same* inclination— viz. not to be put into prison; and of course, though I did not say so, the inclination had to be the same not only in object but also in intensity. Let us now consider a more complicated case where the inclinations of the two parties are not the same. Suppose that, to take a somewhat trivial example (though one which might lead to blows in real life), *A* likes to listen to classical chamber music on his gramophone, and *B*, who lives. in the next room, is considering whether to practise playing jazz on the trumpet.[1] Now it is obviously of no use for *B* to ask himself whether he is prepared to prescribe universally

---

[1] The example is borrowed, with adaptations, from Professor R. B. Braithwaite's *Theory of Games as a Tool for the Moral Philosopher*; but I am using it to illustrate a quite different point.

that people should play trumpets when they live next door to other people who are listening to classical records. For if B himself were listening to classical records (which bore him beyond endurance) he would be only too pleased if somebody next door started up on the trumpet.

The way out of this difficulty looks obvious. B has got, not to imagine himself in A's situation with his own (B's) likes and dislikes, but to imagine himself in A's situation with A's likes and dislikes. But the moral judgement which he has to make about this situation has to remain B's own, as has any other prescriptive judgement that he makes, if it is to have a bearing on the argument (6.9). The natural way for the argument then to run is for B to admit that he is not prepared to prescribe universally that people's likes and dislikes should be disregarded by other people, because this would entail prescribing that other people should disregard his own likes and dislikes (10.5). It does not follow from this that he will conclude that he ought never to play the trumpet when A is at home, but only that he will not think that he ought to have no regard at all for A's interests. Once he is prepared to give weight to A's interests, as if they were his own, there will arise (supposing that A is equally neighbourly) a complicated problem of the sort discussed by Professor Braithwaite[1]—the problem of deciding what apportionment of the time between trumpeting and silence would be just to the two parties respectively. I am not concerned here to discuss this further question, but only to get to the point where it is asked—i.e. to argue B out of an attitude of complete selfishness.

I said that this would be the natural way for the argument to run. But, as before, there are various ways of escape that B might seek to take. Most of them are analogous to those taken in the 'creditor' example, and need not be discussed again; but there is one, just alluded to, which will have to be considered at length, because of its importance for the

[1] Op. cit.

development of our own argument. Suppose that *B* says, 'I am not, indeed, prepared to prescribe universally that people's likes and dislikes should be disregarded by other people; but I *am* prepared to prescribe universally that they should be disregarded under a certain specified condition, viz. when they interfere with the playing of the trumpet—that noble instrument'. If *B* takes this line, he is displaying more than a mere inclination to play the trumpet. For if this were all that he had, he would be indifferent about whether *another* person should or should not be frustrated of his desire to play the trumpet. If all *B* had were a mere inclination to play the trumpet, then there would be no reason at all for him to say of the hypothetical case, in which he, *B*, no longer has this inclination, that *somebody else* should be allowed to play the trumpet. *B* will only take the line suggested if he has, not a mere inclination, but what we shall later call an ideal. That is to say, he must be, not merely wanting to play the trumpet himself, but thinking it good that the trumpet should be played by whomsoever, and that whosoever plays it should not be frustrated, even by *B* himself if he has become so depraved as to lose his taste for the instrument. Such thoughts as these raise problems which we shelved earlier (6.7), and shall resume in Chapter 9.

This apparently trivial example has immense importance for the understanding of some of the most crucial moral disputes. For it is when people step from the selfish pursuit of their own interests to the propagation of perverted ideals that they become really dangerous. We shall never understand the phenomenon called Fascism, and other similar political movements, until we realize that this is what is happening. The extreme sort of Fascist is a fanatic who not merely wants something for himself, but thinks that it ought to be brought into existence universally, whether or not anybody else, or even he himself if his tastes change, wants it. Such a person is very much harder to argue with than the mere self-seeker.

I said 'perverted ideals'. But the trouble is that the follower of such an ideal will not himself admit that it is perverted. And if he does not, there does not seem to be any argument ready to hand whereby we can prove that it is. We shall look more deeply into this difficulty after we have discussed more fully what ideals are. For the present we shall have to be content with the limited achievement of showing that, provided that the trumpeter has only an inclination to play the trumpet himself and not a universal ideal that the playing of it by *anyone* should not be frustrated, we can bring him within the scope of an argument of the 'creditor' type by asking whether he is prepared to prescribe that his own inclinations should be disregarded in the way that he is proposing to disregard his neighbour's. And this achievement, though limited, is not to be despised; for it opens the way to a considerable generalization of the method of argument outlined previously. It can now be extended at will to cases where the inclinations of the two parties differ, provided that we confine ourselves to ordinary inclinations or desires-for-oneself, and leave ideals out of account.

7.2. It goes without saying that our method is still not nearly general enough to cover much of our moral thinking; for so far it can deal only with cases in which the interests of just two parties are involved. In most of our moral problems, not just two but indefinitely many people are concerned; and, though the complications which this introduces make impossible the sort of detailed treatment which we gave of the simpler case, it is worth while asking in a less detailed way what sort of theory of moral argument is likely to emerge if we extend this type of argument to multi-personal cases. Let us, in order to widen the discussion, consider a possible objection which might be made to the argument so far outlined. It might be objected that a criminal facing his judge could use an argument of the same form as we have been using against the creditor and the trumpeter. The criminal might say 'You wouldn't like to be sent to prison, if you were me; so how can you universalize your prescription to send me to prison? But if you can't, then how can you maintain that you ought to send me to prison?'

It must be pointed out in passing that this argument of the criminal's does not offend, any more than does that defended in 6.9, against Hume's Law. For the criminal is not deducing, from a statement of fact about what the judge's state of mind would be in a hypothetical situation, the negation of a moral judgement about the actual situation. What he is doing is to claim that the judge, having a disinclination to be put into prison, cannot accept the singular prescription 'Let me, if I am in the criminal's situation, be put into prison'; and that, this being so, he cannot accept the moral judgement 'I ought to put the criminal into prison', which entails it. And this involves no breach of Hume's Law.

The reason why the criminal's argument lacks cogency is that it represents the situation as being simpler than it is. To begin with, it may be that the judge's desire not, in the hypothetical situation, to be put into prison is weaker than his desire to see justice done even when he is the victim. If this were so, he could, in spite of his desire not to be put into prison, still *prescribe* that he should be put into prison. But this answer does not go to the root of the matter; for his desire to see justice done might have either of the two sources mentioned in 6.7. We must notice, therefore, that even without invoking any abstract ideal of justice, such as would lead him to disregard people's interests, including his own, he can claim that, in this situation, unlike the artificial situation in the 'creditor' example, there are many parties involved, not just two. The judge has therefore to consider, not merely the interests and inclinations of himself and the criminal, but those of all members of society who are affected by his decision. The judge is there as an officer appointed by the community to enforce the law; and, if he does not enforce it, then, quite apart from considerations of 'abstract' justice, the interests of at least the great majority of people in the community will be harmed. Thus a simple argument of the 'creditor' type cannot be applied directly to this case.

It is evident, therefore, that we shall not be able to give a proper account of the judge–criminal case until we have generalized our method of argument to cover situations in which many parties are involved. And a natural way of doing this is suggested by a reply which a judge might in fact make to a criminal, if law-courts afforded scope for such informal philosophical argument. He might say, 'If it were just you and I, then of course I might not feel obliged to send you to prison. But I am considering the people whom you will rob, and whom other people, encouraged by your example, will rob, if I don't put you in prison, and I find it easier to universalize the maxim that thieves should be put in prison.' If he makes this reply, the judge is implying, in effect, that the bilateral argument can be generalized to cover multi-lateral cases. Just as, in the 'creditor' example, *B* had to con-sider the interests of *A*, the one person besides himself affected by his act, so, in a multilateral situation, the agent has to consider the interests of *every* person who is affected. This seems in accord with a way in which we do sometimes argue; but it leaves unanswered the question of how, when we have considered all these interests, we combine the con-sideration of them all into a single answer to our moral problem.

This question could arise even in a bilateral situation, as we saw in the 'trumpeter' case. For even here there are two parties, the agent and one other, whose interests claim atten-tion; and it is not self-evident how we are to balance these claims. We saw that the argument, as set out, could bring the trumpeter to take his neighbour's interests into consideration as if they were his own. But we saw also that this did not, yet, enable us to decide how the trumpeter's time ought to be apportioned between trumpeting and silence. And exactly the same difficulty will arise in multilateral cases: we have to consider the interests of all parties affected; but how does this consideration lead to a determinate moral conclusion?

7.3. An answer to this question is suggested by a further application of the requirement of universalizability; and it is an answer which brings us to a standpoint which has some affinities with traditional utilitarianism. The principle often accepted by utilitarians, 'Everybody to count for one, nobody for more than one'[1] can both be justified by the appeal to the demand for universalizability, and be used to provide an answer to our present question. For what this principle means is that everyone is entitled to equal consideration, and that if it is said that two people ought to be treated differently, some difference must be cited as the ground for these different moral judgements. And this is a corollary of the requirement of universalizability. It must be emphasized that it, like the principle of universalizability itself, is a purely formal principle, following from the logical character of the moral words; no substantial moral judgements follow from it unless the substance is put in by arguments such as we have suggested—and these require other ingredients besides logic, as we have seen (6.3,4). The substance of the moral judgements of a utilitarian comes from a consideration of the substantial inclinations and interests that people actually have, together with the formal requirement that the prescriptions which they prompt have to be universalizable before moral judgements can be made out of them.

Before we revert to the very complicated nexus of interests with which a judge is confronted, and between which he has to do justice, let us consider a much simpler, trilateral case. Suppose that three people are dividing a bar of chocolate between them, and suppose that they all have an equal liking for chocolate. And let us suppose that no other considerations

[1] Cf. J. S. Mill, *Utilitarianism*, ch. 5 (quoting Bentham).

such as age, sex, ownership of the chocolate, &c., are thought to be relevant. It seems to us obvious that the just way to divide the chocolate is equally. And the principle of universalizability gives us the logic of this conclusion. For if it be maintained that one of the three ought to have more than an equal share, there must be something about his case to make this difference—for otherwise we are making different moral judgements about similar cases. But there is *ex hypothesi* no relevant difference, and so the conclusion follows. As before, it is possible to escape from the conclusion by refraining from making a moral judgement at all; for example, one of the parties may say 'I am jolly well going to take the whole bar, and you aren't strong enough to stop me'. But, so long as the three are going to make a moral judgement about the way the chocolate ought to be divided, they will have to say, in the circumstances described, that it ought to be divided equally.

Suppose, on the other hand, that one of the three does not like chocolate. Then they can all happily prescribe universally that those who do not like chocolate should not be given any (leaving out of consideration the possibility that they might be given it to trade with, or given other things in lieu). And so they can all agree that the chocolate ought to be divided in the ratio 1:1:0. It is not my purpose in this book to develop in detail a utilitarian moral system. As we shall see in the next chapter, utilitarianism can, in principle, cover only a part of morality, albeit a very important part. I shall not therefore examine the various possibilities that there are of extending this kind of reasoning to cover more complex cases, but shall content myself with a short survey of some of the main problems that have to be surmounted by such a system.

7.4. First, there is the problem of the commensurability of desires, inclinations, &c. In the main this is a question for empirical investigation, to see whether systems of measurement can be devised, based on people's behaviour in carefully determined situations, which yield results that are consistent, both among themselves, and with our ordinary notions of what we mean by 'desire', &c.[1] To ask for empirical research of this sort is not to deny that much conceptual clarification is also required; it is merely to affirm that it is in the context of accurate empirical research that our concepts are likely to become clear and precise, if at all. We have to attack in this way the problem of the comparison of the intensities not merely of different desires of the same person, but of desires of different people—which is much more difficult. But the fact remains that we all do, in a rough and ready way, make use of such comparisons in arriving at our moral judgements.

It cannot be denied, however, that many and notoriously difficult problems arise, even given that we can compare the intensity of different people's desires. To take one well-known example: suppose that it is a question of giving the last half-pint of water to A or B, and A wants the water though with less intensity, whereas B wants the water very much indeed; but A is dying, whereas B has, in all likelihood, a long life before him. We imagine ourselves in the places of A and B, treating each as one, and neither as more than one; but what conclusion emerges from this exercise?

Are we, in any case, to treat each *person* as one, or each *desire* of a person as of equal weight to the same desire, of the same intensity, had by some other person? The two methods might lead to different results; for there might be two people, one of whom, A, had altogether very moderate desires, whereas the other, B, had many and very intense desires. As a result, it might be the case that, where there was a choice of giving something to A or giving it to B, the desire for this thing came right at the top of A's desires, as ranged in order of intensity, but only in the middle of B's order, and yet that, all the same, B wanted it more than A did. If a sense can be

[1] For a promising example of such investigation, see D. Davidson and P. Suppes, *Decision Making*.

given to this description, we should, if we were treating each *person* as one, presumably give the thing to *A*; but if we were comparing *desires* one with another, simply on the basis of their intensity without regard to who has them, we should have to give the thing to *B*.

Another difficulty is that which arises when we have a choice between the equal but very incomplete satisfaction of a number of people's desires, and the more complete satisfaction of the desires of most of them, purchased at the cost of the complete frustration of the desires of a few. Suppose, for example, that we can make everybody except Jones happy by excluding him from the choir, but that it will make him suicidally unhappy. This will be recognized as analogous to the problem, which has vexed utilitarians, of whether we ought to maximize happiness or to distribute it equally, if we cannot do both. From the standpoint of the present theory it looks as if equal distribution has strong claims of its own.

Then there is the vexed problem about *higher* and *lower* desires, which is analogous to the problem, familiar to students of utilitarianism, of higher and lower pleasures. Are we to give equal weight to all desires of the same intensity; or are we to give greater weight to desires which are, in some sense, morally better? The discussion of this problem has been to a certain extent confused by an attempt to bring within the scope of a utilitarian theory considerations which do not really belong there. If, as I shall maintain, utilitarianism cannot in any case cover the whole of morality, it may be better, when we are dealing with arguments of a strictly utilitarian sort, to follow Bentham in giving equal weight to all desires of the same intensity, irrespective of their object; and to compensate Mill, who objected to this, by the provision which we make, in the non-utilitarian part of our account, for ideals. Mill's mistake was perhaps to try to incorporate ideals into a utilitarian theory, which cannot really absorb them.

A further problem concerns the relation between *desires*,

inclinations, *&c.*, on the one hand, and *interests* on the other. I have been speaking hitherto as if moral arguments could be conducted in terms of either of these sorts of things without making any difference; yet they are certainly to be distinguished. To have an interest is, crudely speaking, for there to be something which one wants, or is likely in the future to want, or which is (or is likely to be) a means necessary or sufficient for the attainment of something which one wants (or is likely to want). It follows that, if we put the matter in terms of interests, we shall have to take into account possible future desires, and the comparison of them with possibly less intense present desires.

Nor is this the end of the problems that arise. Utilitarians commonly put their theories in terms of *pleasure*, or *happiness*, which we have not yet mentioned, though we shall later; it is not evident that an account couched in terms of desires or interests could be easily translated into one in terms of pleasure or happiness. To mention only one difficulty: there are cases in which a man has no desire for a thing (e.g., television) nor ever will have, unless I take certain steps (e.g., advertise television in a newspaper which he reads). If all I am concerned with is the satisfaction of desires which he has or will have without my agency, I may conclude that I ought to let him alone; but if I am concerned with increasing his pleasure or happiness, I may reason that I should increase these by first causing him to have a certain desire, and then providing him with the means of satisfying it.

I mention these problems, not because I think that I can at present solve them, but simply in order that the reader may not think that I am unaware of them, or of other similar ones. I am concerned, not to develop a utilitarian theory, but simply to establish a point of contact between utilitarianism and the account of the nature of moral argument which I have been suggesting. Though unable, because of the difficulties interior to utilitarian theory, to state clearly and exactly what kind of utilitarianism if any will emerge, if the method of argument which I have outlined is developed to cover multilateral situations, I wish merely to point out that the logical character of moral language, as I have claimed it to be, is the formal foundation of any such theory. It is in the endeavour to find lines of conduct which we can prescribe universally in a given situation that we find ourselves bound to give equal weight to the desires of all parties (the foundation of distributive justice); and this, in turn, leads to such views as that we should seek to maximize satisfactions. For if my action is going to affect the interests of a number of people, and I ask myself what course of action I can prescribe universally for people in just this situation, then what I shall have to do, in order to answer this question, is to put myself imaginatively in the place of the other parties (or, if they are many, of a representative sample of them) and ask the same sort of questions as we made the creditor ask when he had imagined himself in the situation of his debtor. And the considerations that weigh with me in this inquiry can only be, How much (as I imagine myself in the place of each man in turn) do I want to have this, or to avoid that? But when I have been the round of all the affected parties, and come back, in my own person, to make an impartial moral judgement giving equal weight to the interests of all parties, what can I possibly do except advocate that course which will, taken all in all, least frustrate the desires which I have imagined myself having? But this (it is plausible to go on) is to maximize satisfactions.

We have, it is true, still to grapple with the 'maximization *v.* equalization' problem alluded to above. But this does not destroy the interest for ethical theory of this link between universalizability on the one hand and utilitarian ideas on the other. It may point to a synthesis between two standpoints in ethics which have been thought to be opposed (though Mill saw that they have an affinity).[1] These are the standpoints of

[1] Loc. cit.

the utilitarians and of Kant, who is usually thought of as a strict deontologist and anti-utilitarian. I have argued elsewhere (*LM* 4.1)—though I did not use those words—that the distinction between deontological and teleological theories is a false one. It is not possible to distinguish between a moral judgement made on the ground of the effects of an action, and one made on the ground of the character of the action itself; it is possible to distinguish only between different sorts of intended effects. If what I have now said is true, it might perhaps be possible to show how the principle of universalizability could generate, by means of such arguments as we have been considering, and given the other necessary conditions, a system of morality of which both Kant and the utilitarians could approve—Kant of its form, and the utilitarians of its content.

    I have, however, said enough to indicate the lines on which a judge could reasonably answer, if challenged in the way suggested earlier. His answer would be divided into two parts. (1) The first would consist simply in a reference to the legislature. He might say that as a judge his job is to administer the law impartially; and he does this if he fulfils two conditions. One is that he does what the law says. The second is that he does not make distinctions between cases that are not different. The judge is here making use of the principle of universalizability; a judge cannot say, without self-contradiction, 'I ought to treat cases *X* and *Y* in different ways, though the facts of the cases are identical'. Since it is a moral 'ought' that is here in question, it is not relevant that the laws themselves are not properly universal (3.3). Justice, as considered in this part of the judge's answer, has two aspects: obedience to the law, and the equal treatment of similar cases. Of these, the latter is purely formal, and grounded in a logical principle; the content is put in by the former. If the criminal has a complaint against the law itself, he should address it to the legislators. (2) Nevertheless, the judge cannot stop here. For if he were convinced that the laws he was administering were wholly pernicious, he ought, like any other public servant in the service of a morally abominable régime, to give up his job. I do not mean that judges have to be able to approve of all the laws which they are administering. Up to a point they are entitled to say that by enforcing the bad laws with the good, they are maintaining the fabric of the law, and that, if they do this conscientiously, the public through its representatives will be impelled to replace the bad laws by better. But there comes a point at which, if the legislative machinery has got into bad hands, and there is no hope of improving matters, a judge will properly decide that it would be wrong for him to remain a pillar of such a régime.[1] Therefore, in principle, a judge—like anybody who plays a prominent part in a régime—can be asked to justify, morally, the régime itself and the laws which it makes. And this brings him to the second part of his answer. Here, no doubt, he will say what I have already put into his mouth, that he and the criminal are two among many, and that it is the business of the legislators to show equal and impartial concern for the interests of these many, treating each as one. And he would have to show that, in making the particular law under which the criminal was being sentenced, they had done this. In this second part of the judge's answer, retributive justice has, in effect, given way to distributive.

7.5. We may end this chapter with two observations for which, because connected with utilitarianism, this is the most appropriate place, although they have no direct connexion with the preceding argument. The first concerns the concept of *happiness*, since this concept plays a prominent part in many utilitarian theories. I have not attempted to formulate my own account in terms of this concept, simply because it is so indeterminate, and has created more problems for utilitarians than it has solved. It must also be emphasized again that

[1] See my article in *The Listener*, 13 October 1955, p. 594.

my own theory of moral argument, as set out in this and the preceding chapter, does not, like most utilitarian theories, profess to cover all moral questions; many lie outside its scope, and therefore, even if it were possible to arrive at a formulation of the theory of the 'greatest happiness of the greatest number' type, this would not have the consequences for ethics which utilitarianisms of this type have been thought to have—it would not exclude from morality those questions which, as it has been maintained, have nothing to do with happiness.

To be brief, we may say that, when somebody calls somebody else happy, there is a rather complicated process of appraisal going on; for the appraisals of both of them are involved, but in a different way. The person who is making the judgement is appraising the life of the other person; but not entirely from the speaker's own point of view.[1] For example, even if I think the life of the typical hunting-shooting-and-fishing squire quite unendurable (for me), I can still call such a person happy if that is how *he* likes to live. Deciding whether to call somebody else happy is an exercise of the imagination—the same sort of imagination as we saw to be essential in the moral argument which we considered earlier (though questions of happiness are not in themselves moral questions). In asking whether another person is happy, we have, before we can begin to answer, to imagine ourselves in his shoes. But here the difficulties begin to multiply. If I imagine myself in your shoes, do I imagine myself having the same likes and dislikes as I have now, only in your circumstances; or do I imagine myself with your likes and dislikes too? Are the likes and dislikes part of the shoes or not? It

[1] I use the more general term 'appraisal' and not the terms 'value-judgement' and 'evaluative', because such judgements as we are considering may be concerned only with likes and dislikes, desires, &c., which, because they are not universalizable (5.4, 9.1), are not, strictly speaking, value-judgements, in the sense in which I have been using that term (2.8).

would seem that often they are (and our previous account depended on treating them so). This is shown by the example just given. I can call the squire happy because, though I do not like that kind of life, he does; and so, when I imagine myself in his shoes, which include his likes and dislikes, I imagine myself liking what I am doing, and not liking to do anything else; and so I call him happy.

There are, however, cases on the other side too. Suppose that we ask whether a mental defective is happy—a man, let us say, who is incapable of enjoying anything except food, and dislikes nothing except physical pain, cold, starvation, &c. Suppose that he in fact gets all the things which he likes and none of the things which he dislikes; are we disposed to call him happy? Should we, as in the previous example, imagine ourselves with *his* likes and dislikes, and, because these are met, pronounce him happy? It is more probable that, although we should admit that in a sense he was happy, we should then say 'Look what he's missing'; and, returning into our own shoes, we should think how much we enjoy all kinds of things like playing chess, which he can never know; and so we should be inclined to say 'He's not *really* happy' or 'He's not happy in the fullest sense of the word'. We have to inquire into the source of this inclination.

It may be that in certain cases it is due to no more than a lack of imagination—the likes and dislikes of the person we are considering are so different from ours that we just cannot think ourselves into his shoes. And so people with weak imaginations may refuse to call a certain person happy when people with stronger imaginations might say that he was. But this cannot be the whole explanation, at any rate in the case of the mental defective; it is not lack of imagination that makes us unwilling to call him really happy. Sometimes it seems that, though we *can* imagine ourselves with the likes and dislikes of another person, we are *averse* to doing so. And this is connected with another fact about these happiness-judgements which can easily cause confusion. When we call somebody else happy, the judgement is ours, in our own person. We can see this by contrasting the judgement that somebody is happy with the factual statement that his desires are in fact satisfied—that he gets what he likes and does not dislike anything that he gets. Let us abbreviate the second of these two judgements to 'He is satisfied'. Suppose now that a person has desires, likes, and dislikes which I very much dislike the thought of myself having. I shall have no objection to calling him *satisfied* if he gets what he wants; but I am likely to object strongly to calling him *happy*.

The people whom Moore attacked for defining 'good' as 'that which we desire to desire'[1] were certainly wrong; but the idea has a certain application, inaccurate as it is, to the elucidation of the concept *happiness*. 'Happiness' does not mean the same as 'that which we desire to desire'; but before we call a man happy we find it necessary to be sure, not only that *his* desires are satisfied, but also that the complete set of his desires is one which we are not very much averse to having ourselves. This explains why, for example, few of us would say that an opium addict was happy (*really* happy) if he always got enough opium. There is a limit to which we can go in putting ourselves into another person's shoes—the limit set by the fact that, in making judgements about happiness (which are in this respect unlike moral judgements), we are not at liberty entirely to extract ourselves from our own. And since what we have to do is to make an appraisal, not a statement of fact, we cannot content ourselves with merely recording how *he* appraises his life from *his* point of view; we have ourselves to make an appraisal, not merely to report on somebody else's appraisal.

Such a report is, however, *part* of what is being said. However highly we appraise the state of life of a person, we cannot call him happy if he himself hates every minute of his

[1] *Principia Ethica*, p. 15.

existence.[1] It is a mistake to treat happiness-statements, either as implying no report on a man's state of mind, or as being nothing but such a report. They are complex; and this explains why there is such an enormous variety in the different conditions of life that people have been prepared to call happy. Anybody who thinks that to call a man happy is merely to report on his state of mind should read a little poetry and make a collection of the different circumstances in which people have been called happy.[2] These different views reflect, not just varying observations of the states of mind of the people called happy—though, as we have seen, their states of mind come into the question—but also the differing standpoints of the speakers. This explains why the utilitarians had so little success in their attempts to found an empiricist ethical theory upon the concept of happiness; for it is very far from being an empirical concept. Without having worked out in detail any attempt to reformulate utilitarianism on the basis of the arguments outlined in the last two chapters, I am unable to state categorically whether or not it is possible to make fruitful use of the concept of happiness in such a reformulation; but I am inclined to think that less trouble will be incurred if, instead, the reformulation is based on the attempt to give an account of, not what it is to maximize the happiness of all parties collectively, but of what it is to do justice as between the *interests* of the different parties severally. Whether such a reformulation would count any longer as a kind of utilitarianism is a terminological question of secondary importance.

[1] It is this factor, and not the general reason which he gives, which precludes the suggestion made in an ironic spirit by Mr. P. T. Geach (*Philosophical Review*, lxix (1960), 222) that the meaning of 'happy' could be explained by saying that to call a person happy is simply to 'macarize' him.

[2] He might try, to start with, Vergil, *Aeneid*, i. 94 ff. (contrast Homer, *Iliad*, xxii. 60 ff.); Webster, *The White Devil*, v. 6, 261; du Bellay, 'Heureux qui comme Ulysse . . .'; Wotton, 'How happy is he born and taught . . .'; and Papageno's aria in *The Magic Flute*, 'O, so ein sanftes Täubchen wär' Seligkeit für mich'—to say nothing of the Beatitudes.

7.6. The second observation concerns a controversy which has occupied philosophers a great deal in recent years. This arises out of the alleged fundamental opposition between two types of utilitarianism, which have been called *act-utilitarianism* and *rule-utilitarianism*. If we adopted the 'maximize satisfactions' formulation of utilitarianism, the two versions of it could be stated as follows—though I shall suggest in a moment that by avoiding this formulation we can ease the difficulty. Act-utilitarianism is the view that we have to apply the so-called 'principle of utility' directly to individual acts; what we have to do is to assess the effect on total satisfactions of the individual act in question and its individual alternatives, and judge accordingly. Rule-utilitarianism, on the other hand, is the view that this test is not to be applied to individual actions, but to *kinds* of action. The assessment of the morality of an action then becomes a two-stage process. Actions are to be assessed by asking whether they are forbidden or enjoined by certain moral rules or principles; and it is only when we start to ask which moral rules or principles we are to adopt for assessing actions, that we apply the utilitarian test. We have to adopt those rules whose observance would *in general* conduce to the maximization of satisfactions, and reject the rest. The merit of rule-utilitarianism has been said to be that it is more in accord with our common moral beliefs than is act-utilitarianism; for we think that, for example, we ought to keep some promises even when to do so would not maximize satisfactions, on the ground that adherence to the *rule* that promises ought to be kept would in general, though not in all particular cases, maximize satisfactions.

I shall argue that if 'ought'-judgements are universalizable, there is less difference between these two theories than might appear. Let us first take some cases with which either theory can deal equally well. Suppose that a man has to choose between two alternative actions x and y. We have seen that, if he decides that x ought to be done, he commits himself, because of the universalizability of 'ought', to the view that in circumstances of this kind an act like x ought to be done rather than one like y. But this is a rule—albeit a highly specific one, and one which it might be hard to formulate in words (3.4). So, unless the argument of this book is totally mistaken, even in deciding on the morality of an individual act by reference to its consequences, as the act-utilitarians bid us, we are at the same time deciding whether to accept or to reject a rule applicable to all acts of a certain kind, as the rule-utilitarians bid us.

There could be only one kind of case which would support act-utilitarianism and be incompatible with rule-utilitarianism. If it were possible to apply the principle of utility directly to actions without the intermediacy of any subordinate principle, then we should have such a case. But it can be shown that this is impossible. For how could it be the case that an action could be known to be such as to maximize satisfactions, without it being known that it did so *because* of the sort of action that it was? Let us try to construct a case in which this would be so. Suppose that I am in a room with three other men, and it becomes the case, as logically as it could, that, for just the space of one minute, the greatest desire of all these men is to be slapped on the face as hard and as often as possible. The principle of maximizing satisfactions might then bid me work as hard as I was able at slapping them on the face, provided that I had no countervailing distaste for so doing.

It might be alleged that here is a case where the action is justified by direct reference to the principle of utility, without any intermediate rule. For, it might be said, nobody can accept a rule that one ought to go about slapping people on the face; and therefore my action cannot be justified by reference to any such rule. But this argument is mistaken. For although nobody would accept the rule as stated, this is not the rule that is relevant. The rule on which the justification of the action is based is that one ought to slap people on the face, *ceteris paribus*, when this is what they most desire. It is true that this rule is a very simple application of the principle of utility; if, instead of 'slap people on the face, *ceteris paribus*, when this is what they most desire' we say 'do, *ceteris paribus*, what they most desire' we shall have, by generalizing it, collapsed our rule into something that is more or less equivalent to the principle of utility itself. If the '*ceteris paribus*' is expanded to allow for the necessary consideration of the interests of other people involved, we shall get a version of the principle that we ought to do what would maximize satisfactions. But all this is not inconsistent with rule-utilitarianism. For this does not preclude the possibility of there being subordinate rules which, when generalized, turn into the principle of utility itself. To find a case which was inconsistent with rule-utilitarianism, we should have to find one in which the principle of utility was applied direct, and in which no subordinate rule was applicable; and this would have to be a case of an action which maximized satisfactions, but not because it was any particular sort of action. It is hard to see what kind of action this could be.

So, then, there cannot be a case which is consistent with act-utilitarianism but inconsistent with rule-utilitarianism. Can there be the opposite—a case consistent with rule-utilitarianism but inconsistent with act-utilitarianism? Such a case would be one in which we ought to act in a certain way because it is required by some rule whose observance in general maximizes satisfactions, even though the particular act does not. The case of promises, already mentioned, might seem to be such a case. Do we not think that some promises ought to be kept just because they are promises, although satisfactions are not maximized thereby? The examples usually given are so well known that I will quote only one, and that summarily. I promise somebody on his deathbed, nobody else being present, that I will dispose his money in a certain way;

it later turns out that if I disposed it in a different way, satisfactions in general would be to a small extent increased. Most people, it is claimed, would say that I still ought to keep the promise. Considerations about causing a general break-down of standards of promise-keeping are irrelevant, because it is not known what I promised. Considerations about the effect on my own moral character can be ignored (for to have a good moral character is to be disposed to do always what one ought to do, and we cannot, without circularity, assume that I ought to keep the promise; if I ought to break it, it might strengthen my moral character to do so). This is therefore a very difficult example for the act-utilitarian to deal with.

The difficulty is, however, to a certain extent eased by the way of approaching utilitarianism which we have adopted. It is most acute for that type of utilitarianism which is formu-lated in terms of pleasure, regarded as a recognizable state of feeling. If we ought always to do whatever individual act would maximize pleasure and minimize pain, it looks as if the promise made to the dead man is of no relevance, because dead men have no pleasures or pains. The same would be true of a formulation in terms of satisfactions, if these were regarded as recognizable states of feeling. But, as we have been stating the theory, this is not what the word 'satisfaction' means. Whether, meaning what it does, utilitarianism can be clearly, consistently, and unambiguously formulated in terms of it, I have not been bold enough to inquire. But I am inclined to think that if such a formulation were successful, it would be by providing an account of satisfaction in terms of the desires, inclinations, &c., of people, and thus in terms of people's interests. And it might be better to by-pass the elusive concept of satisfaction and go to these direct.

The best way, therefore, of illuminating the present prob-lem may be to state it in full in terms, not of pleasures or even of satisfactions, but of desires and inclinations. Now it is true that dead men do not have desires or inclinations either; but the crucial point to notice is that we do, nearly all of us, have many and frequently very strong desires whose objects are states of affairs after our death. *Après moi le déluge* is a somewhat uncommon sentiment. If the average Englishman were asked, for example, whether it would be all the same to him if his wife were to commit suttee after his death, he would certainly protest very strongly and, if there were any signs of his wife wishing to do so, would do his utmost to dissuade her. He would not be moved at all by the argument that, since he would be dead at the time, it could not matter to him.

This enables us to put to the man who is contemplating breaking his promise the same kind of awkward questions that we asked the creditor. Is he prepared to prescribe universally that people should act in this way? By this I do not mean, Is he prepared to prescribe universally that promises should be broken? No such general question is required. I mean, Is he prepared to prescribe universally that in situations precisely like this the promise should be broken, even supposing that he himself is the person to whom it was made? Now it seems to me that he has very good reason to refuse to accept this universal prescription. The reason can be brought out by asking him to imagine himself on his deathbed, in the same situation as that described. Is he prepared to accept the *singular* prescription (which follows from the universal one just stated) that, in such a situation, the man at his bedside should, just to keep him 'happy', make a promise which he is not going to fulfil? Most of us would be extremely averse to being deceived in this way; and we should therefore be very far from accepting the universal prescription which requires it. This manœuvre, therefore, brings the apparently intractable case within the scope of the form of argument considered earlier; and if, therefore, the form of argument is allowed to be in some sense utilitarian, then there is a sort of utilitarianism which can overcome the difficulty presented by this case.

Is it, then, a form of *act*-utilitarianism or of *rule*-utilitarianism? The answer to this question throws even more doubt on the distinction between these two kinds of utilitarianism. It is consistent with both; for what we have done is to show that the individual act of promise-keeping can be defended by the form of argument which our theory provides; but this form of argument requires the asking of a question about a rule. Once the universalizability of moral judgements about individual acts is granted, the two theories collapse into each other in this, as in nearly all cases.

To have a case which supported rule-utilitarianism but was inconsistent with act-utilitarianism we should have to find one that required an individual act of promise-keeping which could not be justified directly by appeal to the demand for a universal prescription for cases *precisely* like this, but could be justified by appeal to some more *general* rule (e.g., 'One ought to keep all promises'), which in its turn was justified by asking 'Are we prepared to prescribe universal obedience to this more general rule?' But we shall obviously not be prepared to do this, if we are not willing to prescribe obedience to singular prescriptions which follow from the rule. So the question reverts to the particular acts; it is these which in the end we have to consider, whichever way we proceed.

If somebody says 'I accept the general rule, no matter what the consequences in individual cases', then he is cutting off morality from its roots. For to accept any rule is, given the way the world is, to accept, by implication, a multitude of particular prescriptions about individual concrete cases. We cannot, in accepting a rule, absolve ourselves from the responsibility for the consequences, in life, of obeying it. To say, therefore, that promises ought always to be kept whatever the consequences, is to commit ourselves to the view that promises ought to be kept in circumstances C_1 or C_2 or C_3, *whatever* these may be, and *whatever* ensues as a result. But how can we thus commit ourselves before we have considered the various circumstances in question?[1]

There is an analogy between a man who does this and a scientist who says 'I accept p as a law of nature, regardless of what happens in particular experiments'. Both are declaring their adherence to a universal proposition without having satisfied themselves that they can accept the particular propositions that follow from it, given the way the world is. The fact that one set of particular propositions is descriptive and the other prescriptive does not make either position less absurd than the other.

So then, if to be a rule-utilitarian committed us to saying that we ought to observe certain general rules regardless of their consequences in some individual cases (and to saying this even before we had examined the cases), then rule-utilitarianism would be, to me, an unattractive doctrine. But it need not so commit us; for, as we have seen, there is a kind of rule-utilitarianism which is quite consistent with act-utilitarianism—namely that kind which, while insisting that its rules be universal, does not insist on their being simple or general, but allows them to become, through qualification in the light of particular cases, both complicated and specific. With this kind of rule- (or act-) utilitarianism I am much in sympathy.

---

[1] This is one reason why we can never be logically certain that we have arrived at a moral principle which nothing could give us cause to modify (*LM* 3.3, 3.6), though we can sometimes be *practically* certain that nothing will happen which would give us cause. It is for this reason alone that we can legitimately (for practical purposes) make it 'a matter of principle' to act in a certain way (3.6).

8 · IDEALS

8.1. ANYBODY who reflects on the moral arguments which we considered in outline in the preceding two chapters is bound to find himself asking a number of questions. Are all possible moral arguments reducible to this or a kindred form? Or are there moral arguments which are quite different in form from these? And are there, perhaps, moral questions in which any kind of argument is out of place? Is it possible that moral questions are divisible into two classes, in one of which there can be argument and in the other not?

I do not propose to attempt an answer to the very general question, whether there may be forms of valid moral argument which are totally different from the ones which I have discussed. It may be that there are. The literature of ethics is of course full of moral arguments of all sorts, some valid and some fallacious; and we cannot assume that no further forms of argument will be suggested in the future. My inclination is to think that all the moral arguments which seem to me cogent could be shown, when reduced to their essentials, to be akin to those which I have discussed; and that the main types of argument which are not akin to these are all fallacious or contain suppressed premisses. By 'akin' I mean 'relying likewise upon the logical characteristics of moral judgements (prescriptivity and universalizability)'.[1] But in default of more

---

[1] One such type of argument deserves to be mentioned—the so-called 'What if everybody . . .?' argument—if only to distinguish it from the type which we have been discussing. In terms of the preceding discussion, the 'What if everybody . . .?' argument can be set out as follows: We elicit from a man that he is unwilling to prescribe that everybody shall do a certain action in certain circumstances; and we point out that, if he is unwilling to accept this prescription, he cannot accept the moral judgement, which entails it, that everybody *ought* so to act in those circumstances. But it follows from this that he cannot accept, either, the particular

detailed inquiry, it would be extremely rash to make any such claim. I propose instead to examine the more limited problem of whether there are any moral questions which are outside the scope of the type of argument discussed in the last two chapters.

The obvious way to attack this limited problem is to look for factors, essential to the arguments so far discussed, which might be absent in the case of some moral questions. Now it is important to remember that these arguments owe their cogency to a *combination* of factors, including all those listed in 6.3 and 6.4; and that therefore the absence of any one of these factors may wreck an argument of this type. To realize this is to be put on our guard against a possible mistake. If we discover a type of moral or other evaluative question to which arguments of this type are not applicable, this shows that at least *one* factor is absent which is essential to these arguments. But it is all too easy to jump to conclusions about which this factor is. In particular it has sometimes been suggested that in an important class of moral questions, which I shall specify shortly, the factor of universalizability is absent, and that this is why arguments of this sort (let us call them for short 'golden-rule' arguments) do not apply to these questions. This suggestion is plausible, because in fact in this class of questions another factor is lacking, in the absence of which the logical requirement of universalizability cannot, as we

moral judgement that some individual person (e.g., himself) ought so to act in those circumstances, unless he alleges some morally relevant difference between the case of this particular person and the cases of others of whom he does not affirm that they ought. And he may be unable to produce any such difference. Thus stated, the argument is little more than a reformulation of that which I have set out above. But there are many other ways of stating it which differ in important respects, and I am not convinced that all of them preserve the same cogency. See my review, in *Philosophical Quarterly* (forthcoming) of M. G. Singer's useful new book on this subject, *Generalization in Ethics*. Professor Singer's book appeared too late to influence my own, but I have been gratified to find so much to agree with in it.

might say, get a hold on the questions; and therefore, because it is not fertile in yielding cogent arguments, universalizability may easily be thought to be itself absent. This other factor is the bearing of a question on another person's interests. If this is lacking (if, that is to say, no other person's interests are involved) universalizability cannot by itself generate golden-rule arguments; but nevertheless the judgements in question could be universalizable in just the same way as those to which golden-rule arguments are applicable. For the arguments would still not apply to them if this other essential factor were absent, viz. the bearing on another's interests.

8.2. It will be instructive in this connexion to consider the position of aesthetic judgements. I shall give reasons for holding that judgements of aesthetic appraisal are, like moral judgements, universalizable, in the sense in which I am using that word—though there may be other senses in which they are not. But it should be quite evident that golden-rule arguments cannot be used in aesthetics. Thus there is at least one class of value-judgement which, though universalizable, is not subject to the kind of argument which we have been discussing. These aesthetic judgements, therefore, will provide us with an illuminating parallel when we come to consider the position of those moral judgements, if there are any, which cannot be argued about in this way. We may be less tempted to deny that they are universalizable, if we have understood that even aesthetic judgements are.

Since many people will wish to reject the view that aesthetic judgements are universalizable, this must first be argued. The opposition to this thesis is for the most part based on mis-understandings of what is meant by 'universalizable'. I will therefore repeat that by calling a judgement universalizable I mean only that it logically commits the speaker to making a similar judgement about anything which is either exactly like the subject of the original judgement or like it in the relevant respects. The relevant respects are those which formed the grounds of the original judgement (2.2). To avoid misunderstanding, it should also be borne in mind that there may be some value-judgements in the case of which the relevant respects include only certain simply specifiable features of the thing (the thesis of universalizability is quite consistent with either *all*, or *no*, value-judgements being like this; both of these views seem to me to be absurd); and there may be other cases in which the features that are relevant cannot be easily or simply specified, either because of the complexity or subtlety of the case, or because we have not become clear enough about the grounds of the judgement. There may even be cases in which *all* the features of a thing are held to be relevant. If there are, it makes absolutely no difference to the universalizability of aesthetic judgements, in the sense in which I am using the term (3.4 ff.).

To illustrate this, I will use an example which I have used before (*LM* 5.2). I shall assume that if it can be shown that aesthetic judgements containing the word 'good' are universalizable, it will follow *a fortiori* that those containing less general terms of commendation are. For these words ('harmonious', for example) have a descriptive meaning that is somewhat more fixed than that of 'good', and therefore it is even less plausible in their case than it is in the case of 'good' to deny that they have the property of universalizability which, as we have seen, attaches to all words carrying descriptive meaning (2.2).

Let us suppose, then, that there are two pictures very like each other. To call one good and the other not commits the speaker to saying that there must be some difference between them which makes them differ in respect of goodness. And if it be granted that there must be some difference between two pictures, one of which is good and the other not, then it follows that if a man calls a picture good, he is committed to calling any other picture good which is exactly similar. Anybody who thinks that all the features of a picture are relevant to its aesthetic appraisal can stop here. But if somebody else thinks that it is possible for some features not to be relevant, he must say that the man is committed also to calling good such pictures as are, while not exactly like the first one, like it in the relevant respects—i.e. those which were his grounds for calling the first one good. The dispute between these two views has no bearing on the present issue, and I mention it only to forestall possible misunderstandings.

Consider the case of two copies of the same lithograph. If the lithography has been consistently done, there will be no visible difference between the two pictures; and, since any difference in goodness as a picture can only be attributed on the ground of some visible difference, there can be no difference in respect of goodness either. There might, no doubt, be differences in respect of some other sort of value. For example, if it were known that one copy was taken by the artist, and another by an assistant, the first might sell for more at an auction. But this would be irrelevant to the pictures' goodness as pictures (their aesthetic value) about which alone I am speaking.

Those who wish to maintain that aesthetic judgements are not universalizable often say that a work of art is 'a unique individual'. This example may help to elucidate what they could mean. Their statement certainly looks as if it were an implicit contradiction of the view that aesthetic judgements are universalizable. But this appearance may be deceptive. Siamese cats are unique individuals—one is never precisely like another; but this does not mean that judgements made at a cat show about their merits are not universalizable. Even if there were only one Siamese cat in the show, a judge who called it a good one would have to admit that *if* there had been another cat in the show like the first one in all, or in the relevant, respects, the second cat would have been a good one too.

8.3. It is, nevertheless, worth inquiring what could be

meant by saying that a work of art is a unique individual. We have to decide whether this is intended to be an analytic statement or a contingent one. We can tell which it is intended to be by seeing what answer is made to a possible objection to it, based on the lithograph example. If, as this example seems to show, there can be two qualitatively similar but numerically distinct works of art, then a work of art is *not* necessarily unique. The first possible answer to this objection is that the work of art is not the individual copy of the lithograph, but some more tenuous entity—the *work*—which is somehow 'manifested' or 'exemplified' in all these copies, in somewhat the same way as a symphony is manifested in all its performances. The person who takes this line is making his view analytically true; that is to say, he is using the expression 'the same work' in such a way that it is logically impossible for there to be two qualitatively indistinguishable but numerically different works. To use the term in this way is to use it as if it were the name of a universal property or type. In this sense, the Water Music is specified and identified as this work of art solely by the notes occurring in its score; the property of being a performance of the Water Music is defined as the property of consisting of certain notes played in a certain order. If someone else were, independently, to write a work consisting of the same notes, he too would have written the Water Music; he would have produced the same work as Handel.

We do not in fact normally use the expression 'work' in this way—though we do so employ expressions like 'theme', 'subject', 'motif', 'melody', and 'tune'; two composers could independently and unknown to each other write fugues with the same subject. It is possible, provided that we are prepared to make sufficiently fantastic assumptions, to imagine cases in which we might be tempted to use expressions like 'fugue' itself, and even 'symphony' or 'work', like this. Suppose, for example, that J. S. Bach sent two of his sons to their rooms with the instruction to write fugues on the notes B A C H, and they came back after some hours' solitary confinement with identical scores, thus showing how well they had absorbed their father's teaching. We might, in these unusual circumstances, say that they had written the same fugue, just as we should certainly say that they had used the same subject. And we might similarly say that they had written the same work; for a fugue is a work and they wrote the same fugue.

That we do not ever have occasion to speak in this way is due to contingent facts about the ways in which works of art are produced. It is obvious enough why different artists do not normally produce qualitatively identical works. More important is the fact that, thus interpreted, the claim that a work of art is a unique individual becomes trivial, and an insufficient basis for the arguments which are founded upon it. We might put this point in a paradoxical way by saying that the work has been made a unique individual only by being turned into a universal. A universal is necessarily unique; for clearly there cannot be two numerically different universal qualities, for example, which are qualitatively precisely similar. With universals, there is no criterion of numerical difference distinct from criteria of qualitative difference. But on this interpretation the view that a work of art is a unique individual says no more than that, since a work, being a universal type, cannot have any uniqueness beyond that which any universal type must have, it has, of logical necessity, all the uniqueness it can have. This is an elaborate truism. To be plainer: if the fugue which Bach's sons both wrote is to be called one fugue, in spite of the fact that two people wrote it, just on the ground that the scores which they both produced are precisely similar, and if this is all that is meant by saying that this fugue is a unique individual, then this premiss, so far from supporting the conclusion that aesthetic judgements are not universalizable, supports exactly the opposite conclusion. If there is a fault in Wilhelm Friedemann's composition, there must be, on this interpretation, a fault in that of Carl Philipp Emanuel; for they are the very same work. And if one is commended, so must the other be, since there is no difference between them. On this way of taking it, the claim that works of art are unique is a covert concession of the point that I am seeking to establish.

If, on the other hand, the claim is interpreted in such a way that it is *not* analytically true, then, it seems to me, it becomes false. Suppose that its upholder, when faced with the examples of the two lithographs and the two fugues, refuses to take the step which we have been considering—he refuses, that is to say, to make his doctrine analytic by claiming that the two works, because they are qualitatively similar, must be 'manifestations' or 'tokens' of the same type-work. In that case, the premiss that works are unique, even if it would support the conclusion that judgements about them are not universalizable (which it would not—see the 'Siamese cat' example), could not itself be sustained, as the 'lithograph' and 'fugue' examples show. We have, in both cases, on this interpretation, *two* works to make aesthetic judgements about, which are qualitatively exactly similar; and so we can ask, Can we without logical absurdity make different judgements about these two exactly similar works? And the answer to this question is plainly that we cannot.[1]

I conclude that aesthetic judgements are universalizable, in the sense in which we have been using that term. It should by this time be unnecessary to insist that this does not mean that there can be simple general rules, obedience to which can ensure the production of good works of art. Rules can be of more use to the artist than is sometimes allowed, as, for

---

[1] This question is dealt with in greater detail in an article by Miss R. Meager (*Aristotelian Society*, lix (1958/9), 49), with most of which I agree. I have also learnt a great deal from a (regrettably) unpublished paper by Mr. Strawson. If, in the desire to make this book compact, I do not pursue the subject further, it is with the hope that Strawson will some time let us have his extremely valuable insights into it.

example, a glance at Thomas Morley's *Plaine and Easie Introduction* makes abundantly clear; but we demand originality in works of art, and there cannot be rules for being original (though there can be procedures for stimulating originality). There is, however, absolutely no inconsistency between the demand for originality in works of art and the demand for universalizability in aesthetic judgements.

8.4. Let us now, having established that aesthetic judgements are universalizable, ask why it is that, in spite of this fact, golden-rule arguments are inapplicable in this field. The reason is that aesthetic questions have no bearing on other people's interests, or, we might add, other people's interests on aesthetic questions. Suppose that a person, *A*, builds, at a secluded corner of a village, a house for himself in the Cotswold style, lavishing care and money on the authenticity of its details. And suppose that thereafter another person, *B*, having bought the only other plot in the lane, which faces *A*'s house, is proposing to erect there a house in the Bauhaus style. Now obviously a great many kinds of aesthetic grounds might be advanced for or against such a proposal; but they would none of them be arguments of the golden-rule type. This is not, indeed, because another person's interests are not involved—for they are; but rather because no *aesthetic* argument can be founded on this consideration. It might be said that *B* cannot claim that it would be all right for him to do what *A* would think completely spoilt his aesthetic design, by which he sets so much store; for *B* cannot think it right that someone else should do the same to him, were he in *A*'s position and with *A*'s tastes. But this, clearly, would be a moral argument, not an aesthetic one.

This can be shown by altering the conditions so as to abolish the possibility of such an argument, while leaving all the aesthetic aspects of the case intact. This is quite easy; all we have to do is to suppose that *B* is the owner of the whole property on both sides of the lane, and has built the first house; then he becomes converted to the Bauhaus style, and determines to let the first house (for simplicity, let us say to a blind recluse) and build himself another one in accordance with his new taste. In this second case, all the aesthetic considerations which could be brought forward in the first case can still be brought forward; for nothing has been changed which can affect the aesthetic merit of the proposed layout —it is still proposed to put up a Bauhaus-style building opposite a Cotswold-style one. There can be, in both cases, aesthetic controversy about the merits of the two styles, and about the aesthetic effect of their juxtaposition. But there can be no aesthetic consideration which is relevant to one case but not to the other; for the aesthetic considerations all concern the appearance of the two buildings, and this is the same in both cases. The golden-rule argument, on the other hand, cannot be applied to the second case, because no other person's interests are affected; this argument, therefore, cannot be relevant to the aesthetic question.

Having reached this point we can see clearly how great is the temptation to say that, by definition of the word 'moral', moral questions can only arise where other people's interests are involved. If we adopted this suggestion, we should be on our way towards a neat solution of the problem of delimiting moral questions on the one hand from aesthetic and other evaluative questions on the other. Unfortunately it does not seem that the problem is open to so simple a solution. It is quite true that a *class* of moral questions can be so defined— namely those which allow of golden-rule arguments. If the word 'moral' were arbitrarily confined to this class, then it could be said that all 'moral' questions (in this sense) could be answered by means of the type of reasoning outlined in the preceding two chapters; and this is a solution which would comfort many. But this would leave us, as moral philosophers, saying nothing about another class of questions to which, undoubtedly, ordinary people commonly apply the name 'moral'. Without wishing to legislate about the use of this notoriously ambiguous word (for that is only a terminological question, albeit one to which some answers can gravely mislead), I wish merely to insist that these other questions be dealt with inside moral philosophy, and not neglected.

Consider the question, discussed on the wireless recently, of whether it is wrong for a pretty girl to earn good money by undressing herself at a 'strip club' for the pleasure of an audience of middle-aged business-men. If this is not a moral question in an accepted sense of the word, it is hard to say what would be. The enlightened may not think it an important one; but there is no doubt that many people think it very important. Yet those who call such exhibitions immoral do not do so because of their effect on other people's interests; for, since everybody gets what he or she wants, nobody's interests are harmed. They are likely, rather, to use such words as 'degrading'. This gives us a clue to the sort of moral question with which we are dealing. It is a question not of interests but of *ideals*. Such conduct offends against an ideal of human excellence held by many people; that is why they condemn it. Even if their condemnation is put in the terminology of 'interests', this is only because, like Plato, they think that to make somebody a worse man is to do him the greatest possible harm.[1] But this Platonic way of speaking should not conceal from us the difference between two distinct grounds on which we can commend or condemn actions, one of which is connected with the interests of other people, and the other with ideals of human excellence. One reason why it is wrong to confine the term 'moral question' by a terminological fiat to questions concerning the effect of our actions upon other people's interests, is that such a restriction would truncate

---

[1] See, e.g., *Republic*, i, 335 c. It was confusion on this point which caused Plato to think that the philosopher-king, by turning people into *his* idea of good men, regardless of what sort of men they wanted to be, would be promoting their real interests.

moral philosophy by preventing it saying anything about ideals.

It is not difficult to find other examples. Suppose that some-body is trying to decide whether to make his career that of a stockbroker or an army officer. It may be that he thinks that, by and large, it will not make a predictable difference to other people's interests which he chooses. If he becomes a stock-broker, he will make money for some people, deprive other people indirectly of the same amount of money, and promote the existence of an active market in stocks and shares, which, it is said, is of service to the industrial and commercial well-being of the community. If he becomes a soldier, he will kill a lot of people, protect a lot of others, and perhaps, if his government's policy is a wise one, contribute in some small measure to the stability of international relations. In both cases there is direct gain to the man's clients or countrymen, and the direct and indirect gains and losses to other people make up, with this, a rough balance, so far as prediction is possible at all. But these somewhat imponderable factors may not be what weigh most with him when he is trying to decide which life it would be best to choose. He may be moved more by the thought (perhaps an unjust one) that stockbroking is a sedentary and sordid occupation, and the military life an active one, requiring courage and self-sacrifice. If on these grounds he chooses to enter an army career, are we to say that he has been swayed by *moral* considerations?

This, as I said earlier, may be merely a terminological ques-tion. But if we say that the grounds are not moral, we shall be at a loss for a word to describe the kind of ideals which led him to this choice of career. And this might make us think that we do need the word 'moral' in this application. But on the other hand it may be that this use of the word is not the same use as when we say that the man in the 'creditor' example was led to reject the view that he morally ought to put his debtor into prison. Once we get away from the terminological problem, the facts begin to look clearer; there are at least two kinds of grounds on which a man might say that the best thing to do would be so and so; one of these is concerned with interests, and the other with ideals. These sorts of grounds must be kept distinct from each other, even if later they turn out to be related in some way; but 'moral' may, all the same, be the word used in our common speech for both of them.

8.5. In order to avoid confusion, let us call one of these kinds of ground 'utilitarian' and the other 'idealist'. A utilitarian might argue that there is a logical (and not merely an historical) connexion between the two, because moral ideals are always framed, and have to be framed, to encourage the development of qualities which will conduce to the furthering of people's interests, or those of society in general. But this is too sweeping a claim. Just as, at Cruft's, dogs called retrievers are given prizes for qualities which are unrelated to their performance as gun-dogs, so many people have ideals of human excellence whose utilitarian basis is vestigial. It would be a hazardous claim, at any rate in modern society, that the moral quality of so-called 'physical' courage is on the whole conducive to human well-being; yet we both admire this quality and encourage the young to cultivate it. This may be only because at one time it was vital to the preservation of society that the majority, at any rate, of its male citizens should possess this virtue; and perhaps, if this is no longer the case in the present state of military science, we may come to abandon this ideal, or to give it less weight. But this is irrelevant to the present argument. It may indeed be that there is a strong tendency for our ideals to be framed in accordance with the utilitarian needs of society in past generations; but nevertheless the ideals are logically independent of the needs, and can survive their disappearance. We must not commit a mistake similar to that which would be committed by an anthropologist who said that the Hindus wash five times a day for purely hygienic reasons; they wash as a religious duty, and though the custom may have grown originally out of vague ideas of hygiene, it would survive the proof that more disease is spread than prevented by it.

Moral ideals have a very close resemblance, in some ways, to aesthetic ideals; they are logically more like them than either are like those grounds for moral judgements which I have called utilitarian. Consider yet another example of a choice between moral ideals in which golden-rule arguments are out of place. The leader of a Himalayan expedition has the choice of either leading the final assault on the mountain himself, or staying behind at the last camp and giving another member of his party the opportunity. Here it is obvious that different ideals will conflict; yet it is easy to suppose that no argument concerned with the interests of the parties will settle the question—for the interests may be very precisely balanced. The questions that arise are likely to be concerned, not with the interests of the parties, but with ideals of what a man should *be*. Is it better to be the sort of man who, in face of great obstacles and dangers, gets to the top of the nth highest mountain in the world; or the sort of man who uses his position of authority to give a friend this opportunity instead of claiming it for himself? These questions are very like aesthetic ones. It is as if a man were regarding his own life and character as a work of art, and asking how it should best be completed.

It may be asked whether, if golden-rule arguments are out of place here, there are any other arguments which can be brought to bear on such questions. Now this might depend on what we are prepared to count as an argument; but nevertheless it is not a merely terminological question. There certainly are arguments that would be cogent in such a case, if the parties already accepted some ideal of human excellence; facts could then be adduced to show that such and such a line of conduct would or would not be in accord with the ideal. This can be taken as read. There are also arguments which attempt to show the inconsistency of two moral opinions, both of which a man claims to hold. Such arguments may make use of the requirement of universalizability; if we find a man making judgements about himself which are quite different from those which he makes about others in similar situations, we can compel him logically either to abandon one set of judgements or the other, or to show differences between the situations. Further, we can seek to show inconsistencies, not between two sets of moral judgements, but between moral judgements and other prescriptions to which he assents. If, for example, as a result of accepting certain singular prescriptions (the expression of his desires), he habitually acts in a way that conflicts with his professed ideals, there comes a point at which his advocacy of his ideals altogether loses force.

Nevertheless, it is impossible, and moral philosophers ought not to try, to find methods of argument which will settle, determinately, disputes between upholders of different ideals in all cases. Suppose, for example, that one man has the ideals of an ascetic and another those of a *bon vivant*. Is it at all likely that moral arguments between them will be such as to compel one of them to adopt the other's point of view— assuming that neither is, by pursuing his own ideal, affecting one way or another the interests of other parties? The moral philosopher who thinks that he is failing his public if he does not provide a logic for settling such questions, would do well to ask almost any member of the public whether he *expects* them ever to be settled.

8.6. We may perhaps go further. Mr. Strawson, in a persuasive paper,[1] has argued for the division of the sphere of what I should call morality into two parts, one of which is concerned with moral rules, its aim being uniformity of practice in conduct that affects the other members of society, and the other of which is concerned, not with morality, in the

---

[1] *Philosophy*, xxxvi (1961), 1.

narrow sense in which Strawson uses the word, but with personal ideals, diversity here being a positive good. I am much in sympathy with the spirit of this paper, and wish to make only two comments. The first is terminological; as I have already made clear, I think it inadvisable to confine the word 'moral' so narrowly. The second is substantial; that ideals can and should be diverse does not, as I hope the aesthetic parallel will have made clear, mean that judgements which express ideals are not universalizable, *in the sense in which I have been using the term.*

This will be better understood, perhaps, if we consider the different uses of the words 'ought' and 'good' in making moral judgements. It is tempting at first to state this difference in an extreme way, and to tie it too closely to the difference between 'idealist' and 'utilitarian' moral judgements. We should then say that, where we are making moral judgements on a basis of consideration for other people's interests, and of the moral principles derived therefrom, we express these moral judgements in terms of 'ought'; but that when we are making moral judgements derived from our ideals of human excellence, we express them in terms of 'good'. But this would not be in accord with the facts. It is perfectly possible for an ascetic person, who is thinking solely in terms of his ideal of human excellence, to say that everybody (or at least all males between 14 and 40) *ought*, like himself, to go for a run every day before breakfast. 'Ought' can therefore be used in speaking of ideals, though it betrays a certain attitude towards them, which I shall shortly examine. 'Good', also, can be used of an act which is motivated by a concern for the interests of others— though here, as I have indicated elsewhere (*LM* 12.3), there is reason to think that the act is called good because it is the sort of act that a good *man* would do; and therefore the judgement is concerned with ideals after all.

Although it is most natural to use the word 'good' rather than the word 'ought' to express our ideals (9.1), we must be careful not to confuse two different distinctions: (1) between judgements about duty, obligation, and the like, and judgements about goodness, perfection, &c.; (2) between moral judgements which are, and those which are not, supportable by reference to the interests of others. I have used the pair of terms 'utilitarian' and 'idealist' to mark the latter distinction. Thus the arguments about 'fanatical' ideals in the rest of this book, though they apply primarily to those who aim at perfection in disregard of the interests of other people, will apply also to those who disregard others' interests in pursuit, not of human perfection, but of some supposed 'absolute' duty (6.7). I have been told that among some tribes of American Indians the ritual torture and killing of captives in tribal warfare was acknowledged as such a duty—even by the victims.

The logical differences between 'ought' and 'right' and 'good' brought out in *LM* 10.1 and 12.3 give us the clue to their different employment. 'Good' has a comparative, 'better'; 'ought', and its closely related adjectives, 'right' and 'wrong', normally do not. Moreover, 'good' is probably best defined in terms of its own comparative (though the definition given in *LM* 12.3 may not be the right one). It follows from these logical properties of the words and from the universalizability of all value-judgements, that, whereas the judgement that I ought in a certain situation to do a certain thing commits me to the view that no similar person in a precisely similar situation ought to fail to do the same thing, this is not the case with a judgement framed in terms of 'good'. For it is perfectly possible for a person to say, consistently, that he is acting well in going for a run before breakfast, but that his neighbour is not acting ill in staying in bed and closely studying the *Financial Times*. For it is not inconsistent to admit that there may be different ways of life, both of which are good. The life of the athlete, and the life of the devoted breadwinner, may both be good. It would be inconsistent to say that each was *better than* the other; but the person in question has not said this. It is only if he is the sort of ascetic who wishes to legislate that others should become ascetics, that he will express himself in terms of 'ought', and thus commit himself to adverse judgements on those who stay in bed.

There is also another use of 'ought', in connexion with ideals, which may seem more harmless. A man who has adopted the ideal of physical fitness, which requires him to run before breakfast, may say of himself that he ought to get out of bed now—or even, if he is weak-willed, that he ought to have got out of bed half an hour ago. But this may be only a hypothetical 'ought'; he may mean merely that if he wants to live up to his ideal, he ought . . . This would not commit him to any moral judgement on those who do not have such an ideal.

So then, our moral language as we have it—universalizability and all—is perfectly well adapted to express the tolerant, diversity-loving views of those like Mr. Strawson. We can with consistency say that there are many kinds of good men and good lives. All we are forbidden to do is to say that of two *identical* lives or men, one is good and the other not— it is perfectly in order to say that of two *different* lives or men, both are good. Our language will also serve to express more rigorous views; if anybody wants to express the opinion that everyone between 14 and 40 ought to run a mile before breakfast, he has the linguistic means at his disposal. For our moral language is neutral as between ideals; and so, therefore, is the philosophy which seeks to give an account of it.

8.7. This distinction between 'ought' and 'good' may also shed some light on the problem of 'works of supererogation', recently ventilated in a striking paper by Mr. Urmson.[1] If a soldier, in order to save his fellows, sacrifices his life by throwing himself on an exploding grenade, he does something

[1] A. I. Melden (ed.), *Essays in Moral Philosophy*, p. 198.

good, but not something which anybody in that situation ought to do. He could not have been called a *bad* man either, if he had not done it—though he would not have been such a good man. And therefore the others were not bad men just because they failed to do it. All the same, he showed himself, in that respect, a *better* man than they. But in other respects (honesty, for example), they might be better men than he. They might even be better men taken as a whole, if he had other glaring defects of character.

It can also be said that everybody ought to be trying to make themselves better men. But there are different ways of being a good man; and therefore it does not follow, from the fact that *A* is a better man than *B* (let alone from the fact that *A* is a better man *in a certain respect* than *B*), that *B* ought to be trying to be more like *A*, even in that respect. For *B* may be trying to be a different sort of good man, and for this it may be unnecessary, or even detrimental, for him to become like *A*, even in that respect in which *A* is the better man. It may be held that courage, the example here taken, is a constituent of most kinds of good character, and that therefore nearly all of us—in particular those who have of their own choice become soldiers—ought to be trying to become more heroic in the way that the soldier whom we have described was. But how hard we ought to be trying depends, perhaps, on how likely we think it that we shall find ourselves in such situations. Perhaps, however, men ought not to reconcile themselves entirely to being complete cowards, unless they are convinced that they can do nothing about it. So, in general, we use the acts of supremely virtuous men as examples, but only in so far as the traits of character which they exemplify fit into a coherent ideal which we find ourselves able to pursue. To this extent the remark about St. Francis in *LM* 9.2 (p. 142) was an exaggeration.

The conclusion, then, of our discussion of ideals seems to be this. Where interests are not concerned, conflicts between

ideals are not susceptible to very much in the way of argument;
on the other hand, conflicts between interests, if ideals are not
involved, admit of reconciliation by means of the forms of
argument which the logic of the moral words generates. The
large question remains of what happens when interests conflict with ideals. This will be the subject of the next chapter.

9 · TOLERATION AND FANATICISM

9.1. In Chapters 6 and 7 morality appeared as a way of arbitrating between conflicting interests. Put as briefly as possible, to think morally is, at least, to subject one's own interests, where they conflict with those of other people, to a principle which one can accept as governing anyone's conduct in like circumstances. But it is more than this: in the broadest sense, morality includes the pursuit of ideals as well as the reconciliation of interests. And although we have suggested that there are some conflicts of ideal with ideal which are not amenable to argument, and that this is no scandal, it would indeed be a scandal if no arguments could be brought against a person who, in pursuit of his own ideals, trampled ruthlessly on other people's interests, including that interest which consists in the freedom to pursue varying ideals. We require, therefore, to look for such arguments; and for this purpose it will be helpful to examine more closely the difference between ideals and interests, and the relations between them.

As was suggested earlier (7.4), we might say that to have an interest is for there to be something which one wants (or may want), or which is (or may be) a means, necessary or sufficient, for the attainment of something which one wants (or may want). Now it is, as we have seen (5.4), characteristic of desires that they are not universalizable. For although it is perfectly possible to have a universal desire (a desire that in a certain kind of circumstances some event of a certain kind should always take place), desires do not have to be universal. To want to have something does not commit the wanter to wanting other people, in the same circumstances, to have it. A moderately selfish man may want to have enough to eat without wanting everyone, or even everyone in like circumstances, to have enough to eat. It follows that interests likewise are not universalizable; what it is in one person's interests to have, it is not necessarily in his interest that anyone else should have.

Because interests are not universalizable in themselves, they fall a ready victim to the requirement of universalizability which morality imposes. It is therefore relatively easy, in principle, to use moral thinking to achieve a resolution of a conflict of interests (though in practice the selfishness of people in the pursuit of their interests often obstructs their moral thinking in the way described in 5.4). Where an ideal is involved in the conflict, on the other hand, the situation is much more difficult; for ideals, as we have seen, have a universalizability of their own, and therefore resist the attempts of morality to reconcile them with one another. This is most clearly evident in international politics. If two nations, or their governments, have conflicting interests, the conflict may be more or less easily resoluble in one of two ways: either by a completely non-moral piece of bargaining, whereby each forgoes part of its interests on condition that another part is safeguarded, and thus safeguards, also, that major interest which consists in the avoidance of conflict; or else by the introduction of moral considerations, whereby each limits itself to the pursuit of those interests whose pursuit by any nation in like circumstances it can accept. If international relations could be conducted in the first of these two ways, there would now, given a moderate degree of competence and clear thinking in governments, be little danger of war; and in the adoption of the second approach to international conflicts lies our chief hope of a lasting peace. But where ideals are introduced into international politics, neither of these methods is so easy of application, and conflicts become much more intractable. The chief cause of the Second World War, for example, was a conflict of ideals between Nazism and democracy; and the chief cause of the next World War, if there is one, will be a conflict of ideals between communism and Western liberalism. If we are to understand these tensions, therefore, it is most important for us to see what, in their barest logical bones, is involved in conflicts between ideals and either other ideals or interests, and wherein such conflicts differ from mere conflicts between the interests of two parties. The chief difference, and the source of all the rest, lies in the universalizability of ideals.

To have an ideal (speaking very crudely and remembering the qualifications just made in 8.6) is to think of some kind of thing as pre-eminently good within some larger class. Thus, if I have a conception of the ideal sports car, this is to think of some particular description of sports car as pre-eminently good within the kind, sports car—I might say, 'The ideal sports car would have precise steering, vivid acceleration, powerful and reliable brakes, &c.' To have a moral ideal is to think of some type of man as a pre-eminently good type of man, or, possibly, of some type of society as a pre-eminently good one. The intractability of the conflict between the Nazis and at any rate their Western opponents was due to the fact that the Nazis' ideals of man and of society were utterly different from those of, for example, liberal Englishmen or Americans. If it had been a question merely of conflicting national interests, a reconciliation might, given patience, have been arrived at by each side saying to itself 'Which of our interests have to be sacrificed in the major interest of peace?' (bargaining); or by saying 'Which of our interests is such that its pursuit by any nation in like circumstances is a principle that we can accept?' (morality). But what the Nazis and their opponents were in conflict about were themselves principles. The Nazis thought a certain kind of society and a certain kind of man pre-eminently good—and it was a kind of man and of society which liberals, with their different ideals, could not but abhor.

Now I have maintained that some conflicts of ideals, as

such, cannot be made the subject of arguments of the golden-rule type, nor perhaps of any other kind of argument that could lead to a settlement in all cases. This was so where no other parties' interests were involved. But the case of the Nazis is different in this respect; for they not only pursued a certain ideal, but pursued it because of the sort of ideal that it was, in contempt and defiance of both the interests and the ideals of others. If the ideals of the Nazis and the liberals had been such that they could be pursued without interfering with each other, argument might have been impossible and war unnecessary (*LM* 9.2). But to have an ideal is *eo ipso* to have an interest in not being frustrated in the pursuit of it; if, therefore, the ideal of one man or nation requires him or it to interfere with others' pursuits of their ideals, or with any other of their interests, the essential condition for living and letting live is absent, and the kind of conflict arises in which argument is again in place and in which, in the absence of such rational argument, violence is almost inevitable.

Let us, as briefly as possible, consider what might be said in such an argument between a liberal and a Nazi. The liberal might try, first, drawing the Nazi's attention to the consequences of his actions for large numbers of people (Jews for example) who did not share his ideals, and asking him whether he was prepared to assent to a universal principle that people (or even people having the characteristics of Jews) should be caused to suffer thus. Now if only interests were being considered, the liberal would have a strong argument; for, if so, the Nazi would not assent to the judgement that, were he himself to be a Jew, or have the characteristics of Jews, he should be treated in this way. If ideals are left out of consideration, there is absolutely no reason why he should assent to such a judgement, and every reason why he should dissent from it; he will certainly agree that it is against the interests of Jews and of everybody else to be so treated. And thus, by applying the arguments of Chapter 6, the liberal might lead the Nazi to reject the moral judgement that it is right to treat Jews (or anybody else) in this manner. But the Nazi has a universal principle of his own which gets in the way of the liberal's argument. He accepts the principle that the characteristics which Jews have are incompatible with being an ideal or pre-eminently good (or even a tolerably good) man; and that the ideal, or even a tolerably good, society cannot be realized unless people having these characteristics are eliminated. It might therefore seem *prima facie* that it is no use asking him to imagine himself having the characteristics of Jews and to consider what his interests would then be; for he thinks that, even if the other interests of people (including his own) are sacrificed, the ideal state of society ought to be pursued by producing ideal men and eliminating those that fall short of the ideal.

A person who was moved by considerations of self-interest, and was prepared to universalize the judgements based on it, but had no ideals of this fanatical kind, could not think this; and it might plausibly be said that a man who professes to think this is usually either insincere or lacking in imagination —for on the whole such fanaticism is rare. But it exists. The person who has ideals of the sort described is not necessarily defective in either of these ways. His ideals have, on the face of it, nothing to do with self-interest or with a morality which can be generated by universalizing self-interest; they seem much more akin to the aesthetic evaluations discussed in the last chapter. The enormity of Nazism is that it extends an aesthetic style of evaluation into a field where the bulk of mankind think that such evaluations should be subordinated to the interests of other people. The Nazis were like the emperor Heliogabalus, who, I have been told, had people slaughtered because he thought that red blood on green grass looked beautiful.[1]

---

[1] I have been unable to find the source of this story, and cannot therefore say whether it is true.

There is another way of indicating the superior strength of the idealist's position. We saw in 6.6 that there was a way of escaping from the golden-rule argument that was open to anybody, viz. by abstaining from making any moral judgements at all. This way of escape, however, involves a resignation from the argument, considered as a moral one; and it does not seem in any way a defeat for the moralist that he cannot get the better in argument of someone who is not competing in that game, any more than a mathematician need feel worsted if he cannot prove that six eggs and five more make eleven to a man who will not make any mathematical judgements at all. But our Nazi is able to perform what is essentially a very similar manœuvre, while still claiming to play the moral game; for he is still making prescriptive universal judgements, and the only difference between himself and his opponent is that the Nazi sticks to his judgements even when they conflict with his own interest in hypothetical cases (for example the case where he himself is imagined as having the characteristics of Jews). In this respect he might even claim to be morally superior to his opponent, in that the latter abandons his principles when they conflict with his own hypothetical interests; the Nazi might say that one should stick to one's principles regardless of questions of interest.

9.2. At this point some philosophers would, I am sure, be tempted to take what seems an easy way with the Nazi. They would say that he is really resigning from the game after all. It is true that he is making universal prescriptive judgements; but this is not a sufficient condition for being said to make *moral* judgements. As we have seen, aesthetic judgements are universally prescriptive, and so, no doubt, are other kinds of value-judgements; a further difference is needed in order to distinguish the species moral judgement within this genus. This difference is to be found (these philosophers would claim) in the very factor which is needed in order to defeat the Nazi in the argument. We have merely to say that a man shows that he is not making a moral judgement if he is not prepared to abandon a principle when it conflicts with the most pressing interests of very large numbers of other people. To put this restriction upon the use of the word 'moral' is to write some kind of utilitarianism into its definition. It is fortunately not necessary to inquire precisely how the definition would be formulated, and whether this could be done without making it naturalistic. We can spare ourselves this task; for not only is any such attempt open to a fatal objection, but, as we shall see, we can achieve all that we need to achieve by less questionable means.

The objection is this. If we give the liberal the victory over the Nazi by means of a definition of this kind, the victory will be in an important sense barren. Both will be left prescribing, universally, different ways of life, and therefore differing about the most fundamental questions that people can differ about. It is not of ultimate importance whether we *call* the difference between them a moral difference, as most people would; or whether, as we shall have to if we accept the suggestion just made, we think up some other term for this kind of difference. This is a purely terminological question, to which we shall return (10.7). What does matter is that the difference between these people should be recognized to exist and that we should do all we can, as moral philosophers, to promote clear thinking about it. We cannot yet assume that nothing can be done, by clarification of the issue, to open the way to a settlement of such a dispute. It may be that there is no way; but we require to satisfy ourselves that there is not. We should be falling short of our duty as moral philosophers if we just left the Nazi and the liberal each playing his own different game; for there is one game which they are both playing—a strenuous and bloody one.

The case is different from those considered in 6.5. Those were all cases in which we adopted a manœuvre similar in some ways to the one which I am now rejecting. It will be remembered that we considered the cases of men whose judgements fell short of being moral (or even, in our sense, evaluative) in one of two ways: either by not being prescriptive or by not being universalizable. In both these cases we, in effect, declined to continue the argument, on the ground that there was no longer any moral dispute between the parties to it. I cited in comparison the case of a mathematical argument with a person who was using the word 'dozen' to mean what we normally mean by 'eleven'. The argument cannot be continued unless agreement is reached on the use of terms; and, once agreement is reached, and *some* term is chosen to mean what we were meaning by 'ought', the argument can proceed on the lines determined by the nature of that concept. It may be asked, therefore, what can be the objection to taking the same line again in the argument with the Nazi. All we have to do, on this suggestion, is to include enough in the concept 'morally ought' to make it the case that he, in refusing to be moved by the considerations that we have brought forward about other people's interests, is no longer arguing morally at all, and can therefore be left to his own devices.

Is this merely a question of how the word 'moral' is actually used in common speech: should we or should we not *call* the Nazi's position a moral one? It cannot be emphasized too strongly that the question that is troubling us is not of this sort, any more than it would be in the mathematical case. Nothing in mathematics turns on the actual use of words, and neither does it in morals (6.5). We could get along just as well if we used artificial symbols for all the concepts involved in the argument; the crucial questions that we have to consider would still arise.

Let us for the moment abandon the word 'moral' as too slippery, and set out the concepts involved more fully. We have then the following concepts, in decreasing order of restrictiveness. First, there is the concept $ought_1$, which is bound by the restriction that one cannot think that one ought to do something which utterly disregards other people's interests, as well as by all the restrictions to which the other concepts too are subject. Secondly, there is the concept which the Nazi and the liberal share ($ought_2$), which is not bound by this first restriction, but has merely to be prescriptive and universalizable. Thirdly, there is the concept $ought_3$, which is prescriptive but not universalizable. Since I do not think that the word 'ought' is actually ever used in the sense of '$ought_3$', I should prefer to use some other word to stand for this concept (e.g., some word defined in terms of 'want' or of the plain singular imperative); but I use the word '$ought_3$' in order not even to seem to beg any questions. Now why, it may be asked, do I put the user of '$ought_3$' out of court so easily by means of a terminological fiat, but refuse to allow anyone to do the same to the user of '$ought_2$' who is unwilling to submit to the restriction which governs '$ought_1$'?

The answer to this objection is that no terminological fiat is being attempted. The questions that are asked in terms of '$ought_3$' are ones which it is perfectly proper to discuss, but which are at any rate quite distinct from those asked in terms of '$ought_2$'. '$Ought_3$' has to do with questions of self-interest which is not universalized—self-interest, and the interest of groups, such as *my* family, and *my* country, which are defined by reference to an individual. For such questions, however, we have a perfectly good terminology, and one which, though it is of interest to the moral philosopher, can easily be kept quite distinct from the terminology which is used for asking and discussing the other two sorts of question. To put the matter more plainly: if all that a person is concerned with is how best to promote the interests of, e.g., his family, let him by all means discuss this question to his heart's content; but let him not confuse this sort of question with that which is troubling the man who asks 'What ought a man (*any* man) to do when faced with circumstances like this?' In 6.5 we were not settling a substantial question by means of a terminological decision; we were distinguishing two substantial questions from each other. And here too we are doing the same thing: questions expressed in terms of 'ought$_2$' are different from questions expressed in terms of 'ought$_1$', and the latter are certainly important. But we must insist that the former are important too; and, if it turns out that to be deprived of the use of 'ought$_2$' would leave us with no way of expressing the difference which is dividing the liberal from the Nazi, this is surely a reason for saying that, even if 'ought$_2$' did not exist, the concept is so important that we should have to invent it, and discuss the questions which are posed in terms of it.

So we may allow anyone, if he wishes, to attempt the definition of 'ought$_1$' (a difficult but perhaps rewarding task). All we must insist on is that, even if the attempt were to succeed, it would leave the ground clear for the important and different question which we have before us. Questions do not become unaskable simply by the invention of a terminology in which they cannot be asked (10.7).

9.3. Let us therefore, for the purposes of the present discussion, forget about 'ought$_1$', and ask instead what can be done, in terms of 'ought$_2$', to clarify the issue between the liberal and the Nazi. In other words, granted that these two are upholding substantially different universal prescriptions, is any argument possible between them? It will be remembered that I was inclined to say, in the case of aesthetic disagreements, that no further argument was possible; and that the ideals of the Nazi are comparable in some ways to aesthetic preferences. Are we therefore to say that one can no more argue with a Nazi than with a man who just likes a certain kind of music? From this unwelcome conclusion we have, so far as I can see, only one thing to save us, and that is that there is still an important difference between the position of the Nazi and the position of the person with marked aesthetic tastes—a difference which we have already noticed. This is that considerations about other people's interests do not affect aesthetic questions as such; whereas the Nazi is operating in a field where other people's interests are deeply involved. The suggestion which we have just rejected makes use of this factor, but there may be other ways of using it which are not open to the same objections. It may be that, even confining ourselves to 'ought$_2$', and not availing ourselves of the more restricted concept 'ought$_1$', we can find a way of flooring at least some Nazis by means of an argument which relies on the bearing of their pursuit of their ideals upon other people's interests.

We have to distinguish, even in the aesthetic case, two things. There is, first, a person's aesthetic opinion about a certain object or state of affairs. But, secondly, there is his attempt to act on that opinion, by way of trying to secure (or alternatively rid himself of) that object, or to bring about that state of affairs or its reverse. For example, it is one thing that I should like a certain picture, another that I should steal it from the gallery in order to enjoy it in my home; and it is one thing that I should dislike a certain piece of music, and quite another that I should cause a disturbance at the concert at which it is being played. So, analogously, it is one thing for the Nazi to think that Jews are inferior specimens of humanity, and another for him to try systematically to exterminate them. It is upon the morality of the latter operation, not of the mere holding of the former opinion, that the liberal and the Nazi differ. It is not, after all, Heliogabalus' taste in colours that offends most of us, but the means he chose of gratifying it.

We have here to appeal to a notion which is at first hard to grasp. Sometimes, when two evaluations or (in general) prescriptions conflict (not in the sense that they contradict each other, but in the sense that, the facts being what they are, we cannot act on both) we allow one to *override* the other. I interpret this term as meaning, not only that we in fact act on the one and not the other, but that we think that we *ought* to act on one even though it involves disregarding the other. For example, suppose that I have in my room in College a scarlet sofa, and that my wife gives me for my birthday a magenta cushion to go on it; and suppose that I am, so far as aesthetics go, vehemently of the opinion that one ought not to juxtapose scarlet and magenta. I may nevertheless think that I ought to keep the cushion on the sofa; because I may think, so far as morals go, that one ought not to hurt the feelings of, or lie to, one's wife.

Note that in order to hold the opinion that I ought to keep the cushion on the sofa, I do not have to abandon any of my aesthetic opinions, or even qualify them. The case is therefore quite distinct from that in which one qualifies, or adds a rider to, a moral principle that one holds in order to prevent it conflicting with some other moral principle that one also holds. Suppose that a man has thought hitherto that one ought *never* to make false statements, but has come to realize that this is sometimes necessary in war in order to observe another moral principle that he also holds, viz. that one ought not, in wartime, to give away vital secret information to strangers. He will then qualify the principle about false statements, altering it to read 'One ought never to say what is false, except in wartime to deceive the enemy' (*LM* 3.6). But in the 'cushion' case I have done something quite different. I have not qualified my aesthetic principle by altering it to read 'One ought never to juxtapose scarlet and magenta, except when this is necessary in order not to hurt one's wife's feelings'. Such a principle would be a hybrid monster, both moral and aesthetic and neither. What I have done is to keep the aesthetic principle unaltered, but to let it be overridden by the (also unaltered) moral principle.

There is a sense of the word 'moral' (perhaps the most

important one) in which it is characteristic of moral principles that they cannot be overridden in this way, but only altered or qualified to admit of some exception. This characteristic of theirs is connected with the fact that moral principles are, in a way that needs elucidation, superior to or more authoritative than any other kind of principle. A man's moral principles, in this sense, are those which, in the end, he accepts to guide his life by, even if this involves breaches of subordinate principles such as those of aesthetics or etiquette. Now most of us, if we had Heliogabalus' taste in colours, would allow this aesthetic preference to be overridden by the moral principle forbidding the killing of other men for such purposes. Heliogabalus did not acknowledge this moral principle; and the Nazis were like him in this respect. Most of us, even if we had an ideal of a society without Jews, would let this ideal be overridden by the normal moral principles which forbid such measures as the Nazis took to realize their ideal. But the Nazis did not acknowledge such principles; in the pursuit of their ideal, they had altered them in order to exclude actions against Jews from their scope. In considering, therefore, what we should say in an argument with a Nazi, it may be helpful to start by asking what arguments could be brought against Heliogabalus.

9.4. Let us first notice that neither aesthetic preferences nor moral ideals could have the bearing that they do upon our actions unless they were prescriptive. Here again the prescriptivity of value-judgements is crucial to our argument. The same point, substantially, can be put in terms of *wanting* or *desiring*, if we use those words in sufficiently wide senses. To have either an aesthetic preference or an ideal is, at least, to want something (e.g., to want not to see scarlet next to magenta; or to want a society free from Jews). We saw above that ideals and aesthetic judgements are not just like desires (9.1); for there is no universalizability-requirement in the case of desires, whereas there is in the case of both aesthetic judgements and ideals. But this does not prevent ideals and aesthetic judgements (again like other value-judgements) sharing with desires their characteristic of being dispositions to action (5.3); and indeed, if we use the word 'desire' in a wide sense, we can say that any evaluation, just because it is prescriptive, incorporates the desire to have or do something rather than something else. The wide sense in which we are here using 'desire' is that in which *any* felt disposition to action counts as a desire; there is also a narrower and commoner sense in which desires are contrasted with other dispositions to action, such as a feeling of obligation (which in the wider sense of 'desire' could be called a desire to do what one ought).[1]

The important thing for our present argument is that, in this wider sense, the Nazi is desiring that the Jews should be exterminated; and, because the desire is a universal one corresponding to an ideal, he desires that *anyone* having the characteristics which make him want to exterminate Jews should likewise be exterminated. And from this it follows that, if he is sincere and clear-headed, he desires that he himself should be exterminated if he were to come to have the characteristics of Jews. And Heliogabalus, too, must, if he is consistent, desire that anyone (even if it be he himself) should be slaughtered, if that is necessary in order to gratify the taste of somebody who likes to see red and green juxtaposed. At least, Heliogabalus must desire this, if he is really, like the Nazi, doing what he does in pursuit of an ideal.

There is, it is hardly necessary to point out, a more plausible interpretation of Heliogabalus' actions. This is, that he has no such ideal, but only a selfish desire. He does not desire that *anybody* (including himself) should be slaughtered to gratify the colour-preferences of *anybody*; he only desires

[1] Aristotle used the two terms *orexis* and *epithumia* to mark this distinction between wider and narrower senses of 'desire' (*De Anima*, 414^{b}2, 432^{b}5).

that people should be slaughtered to gratify *his own* colour-preferences. If his conduct is interpreted in this way, he is open to arguments which we have already outlined in Chapters 6 and 7; and so is a Nazi who is acting from mere self-interest. We have, however, to ignore such people, in order to confine our attention to the hard core of Nazism, if it exists; and to find a parallel to *this*, we have to attribute to Heliogabalus the very extraordinary desire specified in the preceding paragraph—a desire whose fulfilment demands that even he, were it necessary, should be slaughtered to please somebody's aesthetic taste. That we have to look for such a far-fetched parallel as this indicates that we have at least diminished the problem of dealing in argument with the Nazi. For it shows that really intractable Nazis are perhaps rarer than might be thought.

In order to bring out the extraordinary nature of the really fanatical Nazi's desires, let us imagine that we are able to perform on him the following trick, comparable to another which we shall devise later for a different sort of racialist (11.7). We say to him 'You may not know it, but we have discovered that you are not the son of your supposed parents, but of two pure Jews; and the same is true of your wife'; and we produce apparently cast-iron evidence to support this allegation. Is he at all likely to say—as he logically *can* say—'All right then, send me and all my family to Buchenwald!'? And then let us imagine saying to him 'That was only a deception; the evidence we produced was forged. But now, having really faced this possibility, do you still think as you used to about the extermination of Jews?'

The purpose of this manœuvre is to get him, at the end of it, to make—in his own person, as of now—a universalizable prescription in which he really believes. The first stage of the argument is, by itself, of no help to us; it is no good convincing him that a Jew, or a person who believes himself to be a Jew, would make a certain judgement; for Nazis can always say 'Jews can think what they may think, but that is not our opinion' (6.9). But having really imagined himself as a Jew, our Nazi is unlikely to say this. This is not a matter of logic; he would not be contradicting himself if he said 'Jews are such an abomination that I and my whole family, if we were Jews, should be sent to the gas-chamber'. Our argument, as we are going to develop it, will rest, not upon logic by itself— though without logic we should never have got to this point —but upon the fortunate contingent fact that people who would take this logically possible view, after they had really imagined themselves in the other man's position, are extremely rare.

Nevertheless, the position which seems to us so extra-ordinary, when clarified, that nobody but a madman would hold it, can get adopted by a whole people, or by the influential part of it, if the opinion is jumbled up with other opinions, each of which, severally, is controvertible, but which, taken together, form an amalgam which is able to convince. The contribution of moral philosophy is to take this amalgam to pieces and, having disposed of the logically unsound pieces, to display the logically incontrovertible remainder for what it is—something which only very few people would accept. If somebody wants to send himself and his whole family to the gas-chamber simply on the ground that they are descended from people with hooked noses, is there, or could there possibly be, any moral philosophy that could argue with him? Yet this is what he has to want, if, as morality demands, he is going to treat hypothetical cases as if they were actual.

Let us compare the case of somebody who really wants to kill everybody, himself included. Should it disturb us, as moral philosophers, that no argument can stop him wanting to do this, if his desire is sufficiently intense and unshakeable? Should we not rather say 'Well, at any rate, thank goodness not many people feel like that'? This is not an appeal to the principle *securus judicat orbis terrarum* in order to prove a moral conclusion—such an appeal I earlier stigmatized as pernicious (3.9). It is rather a drawing of comfort from the happy fact that most people want to live. We are not saying 'Nearly everybody holds a certain moral opinion, so it must be right'; in moral arguments we are never entitled to beg questions by assuming that our opponent must hold a moral opinion because it is so common. But it is useful to see what can be done in argument, given that the *desires* of our opponent are normal (even if selfish) ones—though if his desires were sufficiently eccentric they might lead him to hold eccentric moral opinions against which argument would be impossible.

9.5. Another objection will no doubt be made to the preceding argument. It will be said that, by using the examples of Heliogabalus and the Nazi, which are very extreme cases, I have rigged the argument in my favour. What I ought to have been doing is to show what is wrong with a certain kind of moral position, taking into consideration only its *form*. By urging that there are, after all, very few people like Heliogabalus or like the more fanatical Nazis, I have perhaps given some comfort concerning these particular cases; but, for all I have shown so far, there may be other moral standpoints identical in form with these, but less extreme in content, which are equally incontrovertible by logic, but which are much more commonly held, even perhaps by quite respectable people. This, if it were true, would be a difficulty for my account of the matter, as set out so far; and it is at least plausible to say that it is true. But though, as we shall see, it is impossible to answer this challenge by showing that the position of a fanatic can be refuted by reference only to its form, we can nevertheless, in virtue of its form *and* of the way the world and its inhabitants are made, do in practice all that is required.

Let us, in order to examine this objection, consider some simpler cases which seem to display the same formal properties. First, let us revert to the example of the trumpeter (7.1).

A fanatical trumpeter, we saw, might be willing to prescribe universally that the playing of trumpets should not be restrained, even if he himself were to develop an intense dislike of the instrument. Secondly, consider how a great many people feel about sexual perversions like homosexuality. They have such a horror of them that they would be willing to, and do, prescribe universally that those who are addicted to these perversions, even if it be they themselves, should be restrained or punished. Thirdly, to be fair, we ought to look at the attitude that very many of us take to drug addiction. Do we not think that even we ourselves, if, like de Quincey and Coleridge, we became addicted to narcotics, ought to be deprived of them and kept under some sort of restraint until we ceased to have the craving? The hope of a way out of our difficulty lies in trying to find some formal difference between the first of these cases and the third; on the way, we shall shed some light on the second case.

Now there is a difference between the third case and the first. Most of us, indeed, think that drug addicts can legitimately be put under some restraints (especially that of being deprived of the drug except in limited and diminishing amounts under medical supervision). But we think that this is legitimate *in the interests of the addict*. To make this case really parallel with those of the Nazi and the trumpeter, we should have to think, not merely that addicts should be restrained in their own interest (for the Nazi does not think that Jews should be exterminated in their own interest; and the trumpeter does not think that non-trumpet-lovers should be trumpeted at in their own interest), but that they should be restrained in pursuit of the universal, quasi-aesthetic ideal of not having addicts about the place. And it is very questionable whether this corresponds to most people's opinions of the matter. Fanatical drug-addict persecutors, themselves, may be as rare as fanatical Nazis. The opinion of the majority proves nothing in moral questions; but it may put us on the track of important formal differences between the opinions of the Nazis and our own opinions.

Why is it that most of us would feel unable to prescribe universally that Jews or drug addicts should be exterminated or subjected to deprivation of liberty regardless of their interests? In the former case it is partly because we do not have ideals which this treatment of Jews would further. But the latter case shows that this is not the only reason. For we do have an ideal of the good man and the good society such that it cannot be realized by a man who is a drug addict or by a society which contains such men. But we, unlike the Nazi, put a curb on our ideal where it conflicts with another's interest. Is there any logical justification for this? It will be remembered that we put into the mouth of the Nazi a boast that he was morally superior to the liberal because he pursued his ideal without consideration of his own or anybody else's interests. The distinguishing characteristic of the ideals of the Nazi and the fanatical trumpeter is that they are made by their holders to override all considerations of people's interests, even the holder's own in actual or hypothetical cases. This is what made golden-rule arguments seem powerless against the determined holder of such an ideal. Let us ask whether we ourselves have any ideals of this sort.

When I ask myself this question, I am inclined to answer that I do not, but that I know of some well-esteemed people who do. We have noticed the attitude of some people to sexual abnormality. The typical liberal will be likely to adopt the view that if abnormal sexual practices do no harm to the interests of anybody, the law ought not to interfere with them —though this does not prevent the liberal condemning the practices as such, if, as is likely, his own ideal of the good life excludes them. He will, to use a distinction that has become topical, think that they are sins (or at any rate moral faults) which ought not to be made by the law into crimes. But there are those who adopt a much severer attitude; the practices, they think, are so abominable that they ought to be prevented or punished even if they are giving satisfaction to the participants, and are not thought by *them* to be wrong, and do no harm to anybody else. As we saw, a person who takes this view is likely to insist that, even were he himself to become addicted to such practices, he should be prevented or punished just like any other offender.

It is possible to think of other attitudes, many of them held by quite estimable people, which share with this attitude and with those of the Nazi and the fanatical trumpeter a certain formal characteristic, already alluded to. This is, that the ideal in question is made to override all considerations of people's interests, even the holder's own in actual or hypothetical cases. Since, moreover, to have an ideal of the good life is *eo ipso* to have an interest in its fulfilment, to make one's ideals override other people's interests is to make them override their ideals as well; for if I pursue my ideal in disregard of all the interests of some other person, I pursue it in disregard of that interest in particular which lies in the realization of his ideals. We noticed in 6.7, as an example of such a fanatical ideal, the case of the man who thought that contracts should be sternly enforced regardless of whether anybody's interests were served thereby. The same attitude has sometimes been taken, by believers in a retributive theory of punishment, to the enforcement of the criminal law. The sanctity of property rights has provided others with a similar ideal. In considering all these attitudes, we must be most careful to distinguish between the two kinds of grounds for holding them which were mentioned in 6.7. If the holder's reasons are of a utilitarian sort—if he thinks, for example, that more people's interests will be more seriously damaged by leniency in enforcing the criminal law than by severity— then he does not count as a fanatic, and we are not here concerned with him. It is only if he insists on enforcement regardless of questions of interest that his attitude falls within

the class which we are now considering; and similarly for the
other attitudes mentioned. It is important, therefore, not to
allow the holders of these attitudes, if they hold them on
non-utilitarian grounds, any accession of strength to their
arguments from utilitarian sources; they must be prepared to
rest their case on the ideal in its own right, without considering any advantages or disadvantages which might come from
pursuing or abandoning it. And it must always be remembered
that a liberal may reject the fanatic's attitude towards the
rights of property, for example, and yet hold, on utilitarian
grounds, that property rights ought to be enforced. We are
concerned, in the argument from this point on, only with
what is left of such ideals after (or if) their utilitarian support
is removed.

9.6. It may help us to understand the issue between
fanatics and liberals if we ask first whether the liberal, as we
have described him, can be said to have any ideals at all. He
is sometimes accused of not having any; but this is unjust.
What does characterize the liberal is that he acknowledges, as
part of his ideal, the ideal of toleration—that is to say a readiness
to respect other people's ideals as if they were his own. Since
this statement is bound to be misinterpreted, it is necessary
to expand it. We saw above that it is characteristic of moral
thought in general to accord equal weight to the interests of
all persons; that is to say, it makes no difference whether it is
you or I that has the interest. The liberal does something of
this sort with ideals as well as interests; but it is important
to make clear just what he does; for he is not, as in the
previous case, *constrained* to do it under penalty of being said
not to be thinking morally or evaluatively. It is true even of
the fanatic that it makes no difference to him what individual
has a certain ideal (for he thinks that even if he himself should
come to abandon his ideal, other people who still held it ought
to treat him as the ideal requires). That is to say, the fanatic
nails his flag to the *content* of the ideal, irrespective of its

holder; and therefore his views are as entitled as are the liberal's to the name 'evaluative' in the sense in which we have been using the term. This, we may note in passing, enables us to rebut the accusation that we have, by the logical account which we have given of moral language, prejudged the issue in favour of liberalism. A liberal could turn into a fanatic without his judgements ceasing to be evaluative.

What distinguishes the liberal is that he *respects* the ideals of others as he does his own. This does not mean that he agrees with them—that would be logically impossible, if they are different from his own (3.9). Nor does it imply that he lacks confidence in his own ideals; the fact, for example, that he would not have 'pop' music banned from all wireless programmes does not indicate that he is in any doubt about his own preference for classical music. In saying that the liberal respects the ideals of others we mean that he thinks it wrong to interfere with other people's pursuit of their ideals just because they are different from his own; and that he also thinks it wrong to interfere with their interests merely because his own ideal forbids their pursuit, if *their* ideals permit the pursuit of these interests. He will be in favour of allowing anybody to pursue his own ideals and interests except in so far as their pursuit interferes with other people's pursuit of theirs. When this point is reached, he will, in arbitrating between people's interests and ideals, give as much weight to each person's as to any other's; he will not give his own ideals and interests precedence because they are his own. It is only when somebody else's pursuit of his ideals or interests interferes with other people's pursuit of theirs that this arbitration becomes necessary; this is the limit of toleration.

The liberal is not forbidden by his principle of toleration to propagate his own ideals; but he is restricted as to the means. He is at liberty to bring his ideals to the notice of other people by all the means that he has access to (but not to prevent holders of different ideals doing the same). He can practise the pursuit of them himself and encourage others to do so, in the hope that this will lead, by example, to their more widespread adoption. What he is forbidden to do is to force his own ideals down the throats of other people by legal or other compulsion, or to seek a propaganda-monopoly, even in some limited field. Such principles as these have often enough been defended by others at greater length, and more convincingly, than I shall have space to do.[1] I wish merely to indicate how this whole topic fits on to the preceding discussion, by asking whether our theory of moral argument, as it has been sketched, sheds any light on the question of how an argument between a liberal and a fanatic might proceed.

9.7. The position of the fanatic has, as we have seen, a certain *prima facie* plausibility. If one has a certain moral ideal (i.e. if one believes a certain kind of man or state of society to be the best), would one not be betraying it if one allowed it to be overridden by consideration for the different ideals or interests of other people? If one does this, can one really claim to be sincere in one's professed adherence to one's own ideal? This is an argument often put forward by fanatics. To it the liberal will reply that the argument of the fanatic only seems to him plausible because he has not understood the nature of the liberal's ideal. It is part of the liberal's ideal that a good society, whatever else it is, is one in which the ideals and interests of all are given equal consideration. It is, to use Kantian language, a kingdom of ends in which all are, at least potentially, legislating members. Since he has this ideal of the good society, the liberal keeps his ideals of the good man and of the good society separate. His ideal of the good man he tries to realize himself, and to win more general acceptance of it; but not to force other people to conform to

---

[1] In one field, that of education, especially interesting problems arise: to what extent, for example, is the coercion and indoctrination of children legitimate? I have discussed this question in a tentative way in a contribution to a forthcoming volume of essays on the philosophy of education, edited by T. H. B. Hollins.

it who have not accepted it, and not to secure its realization at the cost of trampling upon the interests and ideals of others. He may also think that a society is a better one if in it people are thinking actively about ideals of human excellence; and this involves some experimentation and the simultaneous pursuit of different ideals of human excellence by different people. He does not claim finality for his own ideal, though he may be sure that it is the best that he has so far discovered.

He may even think that a diversity of ideals is in itself a good thing, not only because people are different and what they are likely to succeed in achieving is different (it is sheer waste when a man who could have been an artist of genius becomes an indifferent civil servant—and vice versa) but also because 'it takes all sorts to make a world' (8.6). If the liberal's ideal is of any of these kinds, he is not betraying it but following it if he tolerates other people's pursuit of their ideals, provided that, where the pursuit of one ideal hinders the pursuit of another, there shall be, as in the cases of conflicting interests discussed above, a just distribution of advantages and disadvantages. It is only the last proviso which prevents the liberal from allowing even the fanatic to pursue his ideals without impediment; but the liberal is not required by his own ideal to tolerate intolerance. Perhaps the foregoing discussion will have made clearer the logical basis of the liberal's position on this much-discussed question.

9.8. In his war with the fanatic, the best strategy for the liberal to adopt is one of persistent attrition. For there are, as we have seen, certain weapons available to him, in the nature of moral thought, which, if he keeps fighting and does not lose heart, will cause all but a small hard core of fanatics to relent. His aim should be to reduce this hard core in numbers as much as he can. He will be successful in this aim, if he can induce ordinary members of the public, first to be clear about the logical properties of the moral words, as we have described them; secondly to inform themselves about the facts concerning whatever question is in dispute; and thirdly to exercise their imaginations. The first of these requirements is the province of the philosopher; and since the whole of this book has been concerned with it, we may leave it for a moment and consider the other two. To make people well informed is the task of social and other scientists, historians and, in another way, of journalists and their like. To cause people to exercise their imaginations is above all the task of the artist—especially the novelist and the dramatist. These latter have, it goes without saying, other claims on their skill, which have nothing to do with moral thinking, but arise from their pursuit of artistic perfection for its own sake. Their contributions to moral thought may not even make them any better artists; but, so far as moral thinking goes, this is their main role. Many examples from the present day spring to mind; I will mention only one, which may not spring to mind, because it achieved its purpose before the Second World War, and may therefore have been by now forgotten by most people. Sir Alan Herbert, in the course of his protracted campaign for the liberalization of the divorce laws, wrote a novel called *Holy Deadlock*, which was a sympathetic account of the tribulations of some unhappy people caught up in them. The effectiveness of this novel as an argument for a liberal position depended on its power to awaken the sympathetic imaginations of its readers.

By contrast, the fanatic cannot so successfully avail himself of these weapons. It is true that the study of philosophy, *by itself*, may leave his fanaticism unimpaired; it is, however, a useful and even necessary adjunct to the liberal's arguments, as displaying their form (6.4, 11.9). The other weapons, too, may be found in the hands of the fanatic; but they are less effective than when employed by his opponents. The fanatic may, indeed, recruit social scientists, historians, and journalists who will say what furthers his cause; but they will do this only by careful selection of the facts they relate—by *suppressio veri* and perhaps worse. That is why it is so important for the liberal to insist—in despite of some philosophers of history who have served in the fanatical army—that there is such a thing as publicly ascertainable historical truth. Novelists and dramatists also are open to a similar danger; for it is of the essence of successful story-telling to concentrate on certain aspects of the fictional situation, and so neglect others; and it is therefore possible for a novelist to hide from the imaginations of his readers such human sufferings as would result from the observance of the fanatic's principles, and to emphasize instead, for example, the heroism of the typical fanatic. But, provided that the fanatical party is not able to employ censorship, or to control the means of communication in other ways, it will be at a disadvantage in these exchanges. This is because that part of the public which thinks at all seriously and thoroughly about these matters is already well-enough informed, by its own unaided observation, of what is likely to happen in certain kinds of situation (of what it is like to be bereaved, for example), to be able to tell when journalism or history or social science or story-telling have turned into propaganda. And this is why fanatics always have recourse to some kind of censorship when they can, and why their appeal is so often directed chiefly to those who do not think seriously or thoroughly.

For not only factual writing, but even imaginative literature, is subject in a sense to truth-conditions. I have claimed that the sympathetic imagination plays an important part in moral thought; and it therefore becomes most important to make it clear that truth and falsehood are involved even in the exercise of the imagination. In real life, as opposed to literature, it is obvious that there is a difference between imagining the sufferings of a person who really is suffering, and imagining that a person is suffering when really he is not. Suppose that a child imagines that a person who is pruning a fruit-tree is causing it terrible suffering, and is therefore a wicked, cruel man. And suppose that the child is then convinced by an explanation of the structure of the tree that, because it has no nervous system, it cannot feel pain (philosophical difficulties about the justification for the child's change of belief do not now concern us (11.2)). The child will then no doubt withdraw its previous adverse moral judgement on the pruner, having lost the factual ground of it; though he can still imagine what it would be like for the tree to have a nervous system and to feel pain, he has now been convinced that in fact no pain is felt. What this example shows is that to imagine the real sufferings of another sentient being is to confront the facts—and it makes a difference, as always, that they should really be facts.

The same holds good, with a necessary qualification, of situations described in imaginative literature, when this is used as an adjunct to moral thought. It is true that these situations are not represented as actually occurring; but they are claimed to be like situations which do occur—otherwise their relevance to moral thought would be small. If therefore the reader senses that the descriptions lack verisimilitude, or that in an actual situation there would be morally relevant features which are suppressed in the story, the influence of the story on his moral thinking will be, rightly, diminished thereby. That is why it is very important not to take all the examples in one's moral thinking out of fiction, as the young and those who have led sheltered lives are apt to do. For story-books, though they help to stimulate our imaginations, do not by themselves help us, very much, to separate what is really likely to happen from what is not, nor to assess the probable frequency of its occurrence. For this, some experience of actual moral perplexities, and of the actual consequences of certain moral choices, is a necessity. A few months spent as a coolie building the Burma railway is worth more to one's moral thinking than the reading of a great many novels or even factual reports about underdeveloped countries.

These considerations may explain why, on the whole (though there are set-backs) liberalism advances against fanaticism, provided that there is freedom of communication, and that the influential part of the public thinks seriously about moral questions, understands their nature, and respects the truth. The liberal should therefore above all struggle to preserve these conditions; and that is why it is important to the liberal that the moral philosopher, who is professionally concerned in preserving them (especially the second), should do his job properly. Fanatics will always be with us. If there are people so wedded to some fanatical ideal that they are able to imagine, in their full vividness, the sufferings of the persecuted, and who can still prescribe universally that this persecution should go on in the service of their ideals, even if it were they themselves who had to suffer thus, then they will remain unshaken by any argument that I have been able to discover. And it seems that there will always be such people —few, perhaps, who go to the lengths of persecution reached by the Nazis, or by some religious persecutors; but more who take what is formally a similar attitude to the less violent and wholesale kinds of persecution. The numbers of these fanatics, however, will be shown to be small if we insist that nobody can be enrolled among them merely on the score that he has not exercised his imagination, or taken pains to discover the truth. The strategy of the liberal must be to separate from the true fanatics, whose ideals really are proof against the ordeal by imagination and the facts, those who support them merely because they are thoughtless and insensitive.

But there is likely to remain a hard core of fanatics. Does its existence impugn our whole account of moral reasoning? This depends on what we are looking for. If our aim were purely theoretical, to produce a watertight method of argument which would force people to the same moral conclusions whatever the world and the people in it were like, then we should have to admit failure. But perhaps a humbler aim is all that we should aspire to. If we can show that there is a form of argument which, without assuming any antecedent moral premises, but given that people are as they are and the world as it is, will lead them (provided that they will think morally and exercise their imaginations, and will face the facts, and take pains to understand what they are saying) to agree upon certain moral principles which are conducive to the just reconciliation of conflicting interests, then we shall have done, perhaps, all that is required. That there will always be fanatics must be admitted; but it can also be admitted that the true fanatics are relatively few, and would have no power at all to do harm, were it not for their ability to mislead, and thus win the support of, large numbers of people who are not themselves fanatics. This they do by concealing facts and spreading falsehoods; by arousing passions which will cloud the sympathetic imagination—in short by all the familiar methods of propaganda. These methods would have less power over people if one essential condition for their success were removed: confused thinking. If a person understands clearly what he is doing when he is asking a moral question and answering it, and understands just how facts enter into moral arguments; if he is able to distinguish genuine facts from those 'facts' which are really concealed evaluations; if, in short, he is clear-headed enough to stick to the moral question that he is asking and to set about answering it in the way that its nature demands; then the propagandist will have little power over him. To arm people in this way against propaganda is the function of moral philosophy.

PART III

FROM THEORY TO PRACTICE

By their fruits ye shall know them.

ST. MATTHEW, VII, 20.

10 · LOGIC AND MORALS

10.1. IF experience in oral discussion is any guide, there is a question concerning what I have been saying which, if I do not discuss it at some length, will continue to trouble the reader. It is a question which has, indeed, been answered by implication in what has gone before, and to which I have from time to time explicitly referred; the present chapter is therefore not, in any sense, an afterthought, or attempt to remedy a weakness which has become apparent. What I shall say could be said for himself by a reader who has understood what he has read in the preceding chapters; but I have become cautious enough to wish to make the matter, if I can, even clearer.

I refer to the question of the relation between ethics, considered as a study of the logical character of moral concepts or words, and substantive moral questions. The question can best be approached by examining certain objections which are frequently made to the sort of thing that I have been saying. The essence of all of them is that I am trying to eat my cake and have it. I have been in the past, and still am, a stout defender of Hume's doctrine that one cannot deduce moral judgements from non-moral statements of fact; and also of that particular application of the doctrine which says that one cannot deduce moral judgements of substance from

statements about the uses of words or about the logical relations between concepts. Yet I have not drawn the conclusion
from this thesis which so many have drawn, namely that the
only kind of cogent moral argument is one which has as
a premiss a moral principle already accepted by both parties
to the argument. On the contrary, I have maintained that,
once the logical character of the moral concepts is understood,
there can be useful and compelling moral argument even
between people who have, before it begins, no substantive
moral principles in common.

Let us consider various forms of this objection. It may be
said, first of all, that I am open to the same sort of attack as
I, and those of like opinion, bring against the naturalists. The
essence of naturalism is to say 'If you understand the meaning of such and such a moral word, you cannot deny such and
such a moral assertion'. It will certainly be objected that I
have been saying this very thing. The most fundamental
objection against naturalism is that it makes moral questions
depend upon conceptual ones—whereas we feel that to adopt
a certain conceptual apparatus is one thing, and to adopt a
certain system of moral principles another (2.7), though there
are some concepts which we shall not employ unless our
moral principles are of a certain stamp. Consider again, for
example, the thesis, typical of recent naturalists, that at any
rate the more specialized moral words like 'courageous' (on
which they are inclined to fix their attention) are tied by their
meaning to certain evaluations *and* to certain descriptions—
thus firmly tying the evaluations to the descriptions. If, they
say, one does not evaluate highly a certain kind of acts, then
one will just have to give up using the word 'courageous'.
Conversely, if one continues to use the word, that commits
one to certain evaluations. If a man, in a battle, deliberately disregards his own safety in order to preserve that of his fellow
soldiers, one cannot, if one has the word in one's vocabulary, deny that he has been courageous. But 'courageous' is,

by its very meaning, a term of commendation; therefore, by using it, one expresses a favourable evaluation of the act. So, once we have this word or concept in use, we are led ineluctably, despite Hume, from a description to an evaluation.

We shall not, however, be so attracted by this naturalist argument if we take as an example, not a concept which incapsulates evaluations that we are all disposed to make, but one incapsulating attitudes which most of us abhor. Consider an example used earlier—the word 'nigger'. A naturalist might put forward an argument, identical in form with the one just summarized, to show that we have to despise negroes. If, he might argue, a man has curly hair and a black skin and thick lips, and is descended from people with similar features, then we cannot deny that he is a nigger. But 'nigger' is a term of contempt. Therefore, if we have the word 'nigger' in use, we are led ineluctably from factual propositions about his skin-colour, &c., to the indubitably evaluative proposition that he is a nigger. If one knows that he has a black skin, &c., one cannot but (*logically* cannot but) despise him.

To this argument, a person who is not inclined to despise people just because they are negroes will reply that, simply because the user of the word 'nigger' is led along this path, *he* prefers not to use the word 'nigger'. By abandoning the concept, he becomes no longer committed to the attitude. He substitutes, let us suppose, the neutral word 'negro'. Then, though he cannot deny that the man with black skin, &c., is a negro, this does not commit him to thinking of him as inferior.

The only reason why such a course with the word 'courageous' would seem to us strange is that we are, most of us, very firmly wedded to the attitude which the word incapsulates. *If* there were a person who was not in the least disposed to commend those who preserved the safety of others by disregarding their own, then he could say, as before, 'I prefer not to use the word "courageous", just because it incapsulates this attitude to which I do not subscribe. I prefer the longer, morally neutral expression, "disregarding one's own safety in order to preserve that of others". This, though it is not equivalent to "courageous", even descriptively, is in fact all that we can be logically compelled to admit of a person, once he has done the "courageous" act referred to. To go on to call the act courageous is, strictly speaking, an additional step which I am not disposed to take, because I do not share the evaluations of those who take it. It is true that there is no single evaluatively neutral word, like "negro", which in the present case can be used to describe such actions without committing the describer to any evaluation; but we *could* have such a word. What I shall actually do, in default of an invented word, is to use the same word "courageous", but to make it clear by my tone of voice or by putting quotation marks round it, that I am using it in a purely descriptive sense, implying thereby no commendation whatever.'[1]

10.2. We must note that it is secondarily evaluative words (2.7) which occur most naturally in arguments of the type which we have been considering—that is to say, words which have their descriptive meaning more firmly tied to them than their evaluative. Naturalists have sometimes sought to maintain that the same sort of argument could by analogy be extended to the more general moral words like 'good'; but we must be careful to notice just what is happening in such extensions. We have these more general, primarily evaluative words just because we do not want to be the prisoners of our

[1] For an example of an analogous, though more intricate, manœuvre with the word 'blasphemous' during Oscar Wilde's libel action, see W. Gaunt, *The Aesthetic Adventure* (Cape, 1945), pp. 150 f. (Penguin, 1957, pp. 181 f.). The jury, which shared the evaluations incapsulated in the word, was easily convinced, on the facts, that a certain story was blasphemous; Wilde, however (though he condemned the story on other grounds), could not be compelled to agree to the sort of condemnation implied by 'blasphemous', it not being 'a word of his'. The whole book is to be recommended as a storehouse of examples apposite to the present topic.

own conceptual apparatus. If a man wishes to reject the evaluations which are incapsulated in the word 'nigger', he can do so explicitly by using another value-word—often a more general one; he may say 'A man can be a negro, and be none the *worse* for that'. Here the value-word 'worse', just because it is not tied to any particular evaluative attitude, can be used to reject the one to which the word 'nigger' is tied. Similarly a man might say, 'Blasphemy is sometimes a duty', indicating by his tone or by the context that he was using the word 'blasphemy' in a purely descriptive way. And in the same fashion a man who did not believe in sacrificing his own safety to that of others might say 'It's wrong to indulge in these heroics; a man's first duty is to himself'.

The naturalist is, nevertheless, quite right if he claims that what can easily happen to the word 'nigger' can be made to happen, though with more reluctance, even to the most general value-words. If the evaluations which are expressed by a certain word are so unanimous in a given society that its descriptive meaning gets very firmly tied to it (the evaluation comes to be incapsulated in the word), then, even if it is a general word like 'good', it can either 'get into inverted commas' or become 'conventional' (*LM* 7.5, 9.3). Since, however, it is always, even with the most general value-words, open to anyone who rejects the evaluation that is incapsulated in a word to go on using the word, but in inverted commas, it is never the case, as naturalists seem to claim that it is, that our mere possession of a certain word commits us to certain evaluations. It is true that, given that a word has, through the unanimity of people's evaluations, got a certain descriptive meaning very securely tied to it, it is possible to derive judgements containing the word from non-evaluative statements; but, if this is done, nobody can be compelled logically to accept the *evaluation* which is normally incapsulated in the word; he can only be compelled to accept what is implied in the *descriptive* meaning of the word. Thus, though what is normally a value-word occurs in the conclusion of the natural-ist's argument, the victory is barren, since the evaluation can always be down-graded so that it becomes no evaluation at all, but a mere repetition of the premiss; and this, indeed, is all that was really entailed by the original description.

The upshot is that the mere existence of a certain con-ceptual apparatus cannot compel anybody to accept any par-ticular evaluation, although it is more difficult to break away from evaluations which are incapsulated in the very language which we use—hence the potency of Newspeak (2.7). For we can, at any rate in this respect, *alter* our conceptual apparatus —by treating as descriptive a word which used to be evalua-tive. It follows that the insights of the naturalists are not sufficiently fundamental to give us help when we are in doubt about accepting the evaluations which are incapsulated in our language. To a southerner who was in process of breaking away from the attitude towards negroes current in his society, it would be unhelpful to appeal to the word 'nigger' to ease his doubts. If his doubts still persist and grow, and he comes to think that negroes are the equals of whites, the word 'nigger' will be the first casualty. Word-usage can delay changes in attitudes; it cannot postpone them indefinitely. And the same would be true if we came to alter our attitude to actions that are now called 'courageous', or even to those now called 'duties'. If the attitudes go, the vocabulary will go, or lose its evaluative meaning, or acquire a new descriptive meaning (*LM* 7.4 ff.).

10.3. The line of attack which I have adopted against this naturalist argument will have surprised nobody. My purpose in saying again what I have said already is to make it clear why I have to answer the objection to which I referred at the beginning of this chapter. Is it not true that I, too, am trying to make language do a job that it cannot do? Am I not, as I have implied that the naturalists are, taking a verbal victory for a real one? May it not be that the particular conceptual

apparatus that I am using—that of value-judgements interpreted as universal prescriptions—has been adopted by me
simply because it incapsulates my own attitudes and evaluations? A suggestion has even been made about the content of
the attitudes that are incapsulated in the concepts of people
like myself. It is said that we, because we are 'liberals' and
'protestants', have written into the logic of moral language,
as we interpret it, some features which merely reflect our own
moral attitudes. We have (as I have accused the naturalists of
doing) recommended the adoption of a language in which
only our own opinions can be expressed without logical
absurdity—or at least one in which different opinions from
ours are indefensible. And the recommendation, it is implied,
has been pressed by the false and dishonest claim that moral
words are already used, by all men, in the way in which *we*
want them to be used. The truth is, however (so it is alleged),
that only liberals and protestants like ourselves—and extreme
ones at that—use words in this way; the greater part of mankind uses them in quite different ways. Is it we, then, who
are inventing a Newspeak?

Now there is this much of truth in these allegations, that
I am a liberal and a protestant, in some senses of those words
—it would take a long time to explain in what senses. But it
is simply not true that the things which I have said about the
logic of moral language are peculiarly tied to any particular
moral standpoint. To say that moral and other value-judgements are prescriptive and universalizable is not, by that
alone, to commit oneself to any particular moral opinion. By
allowing that a sufficiently fanatical Nazi, who was really prepared to immolate himself in the service of his ideal, could
not be touched by my arguments, I at least guarded myself
against *this* allegation. Although I am a liberal and a protestant, what I have said about moral language could be accepted
by somebody who was as illiberal and as counter-reforma-
tionary as could be. For example, the judgement that one

ought always to do exactly what is said by a person in a clerical collar (or wearing a badge of superior military rank), no matter what it is, can be a prescriptive and universal judgement; yet it is not likely to be accepted by liberals or protestants.

But, it may be asked, how, if my views about the logic of moral discourse do not commit me to any particular moral views, have I been able to erect the elaborate structure of moral reasoning of the preceding chapters, which claims to be relevant to moral issues, and indeed to lead in many cases to the settlement of them? This must surely be a conjuring-trick, because I have produced moral arguments out of nothing but factual and verbal premisses, which is the very thing that I have claimed to be impossible.

10.4. The answer to this attack is that the type of moral reasoning which I have been recommending is, though all the inferences which it contains are strictly deductive, not of the usual premisses-to-conclusion sort like that recommended by the naturalists (6.1,2). Naturalists put forward arguments of the form that is typified by 'He's black; so he's a nigger; so he's inferior'. The kind of argument which I have been recommending is rather a kind of exploration. We are to go about looking for moral judgements which we can both accept for our own conduct and universalize to cover the conduct of other actual or hypothetical people. What prevents us from accepting certain moral judgements which are perfectly formulable in the language is not logic alone, but the fact that they have certain logical consequences which we cannot accept—namely certain singular prescriptions to other people in hypothetical situations. And the 'cannot' here is not a logical 'cannot' (6.9). It would not be self-contradictory to accept these prescriptions; but all the same we cannot accept them except on one condition which is most unlikely to be fulfilled—namely that we should become what I have called 'fanatics'.

Consider, for example, the generalized form of the argument in 7.1, in which the 'trumpeter' example was used as an illustration. The reason why the trumpeter, unless he were a fanatic, would be willing to accord weight to the inclinations of his neighbour is this. He himself is unwilling to prescribe universally that people's desires should be disregarded, because to prescribe this would be to prescribe the disregarding of his own desires. But if he wishes to say that he ought to disregard his neighbour's desires on this occasion, he has either to prescribe in general that people's desires should be disregarded (and this, as we have seen, he will be unwilling to do) or to prescribe that people's desires should be disregarded under certain conditions, specified without reference to *whose* desires they are.

Now, as we saw, it is open to him to say 'The desires of people ought always to be disregarded when they interfere with the playing of the trumpet'. To say this is to take the sort of line which we described as 'fanatical'; and if it is taken, the argument will follow the course outlined in 9.4, and it will be possible for the fanatical trumpeter, at a certain price, to avoid our arguments. But if he is not a fanatic, and is guided solely by self-interest, together with a willingness to universalize the maxims which it suggests, then he will not be willing to prescribe that even he himself, were he to come to dislike the trumpet, should have his dislike of it disregarded by his neighbours. So the condition which he has to add, to qualify the general prescription that people's desires should be disregarded, cannot be that they should be disregarded if this is necessary *in order that the trumpet may be played*. What other conditions, then, can be added in order to make the prescription acceptable to him? The answer seems to be, Only those prescriptions which he is prepared to accept as applying to an act perpetrated against himself, were his desires to change and come to be of the same sort as those which his neighbour now has. To put the point in another way: unless he is prepared to disregard anybody's desires, even his own, when they conflict with a certain end (and this alternative, fanaticism, we have supposed him unwilling to take), he is compelled to give weight to his neighbour's desires—the same weight as he is willing to give to his own hypothetical desires, were he to have those which his neighbour now has.

Now it will be noticed that this dilemma has been stated purely formally. It does not matter what the desires in question are. This gives the clue to the difference between my position and that of the naturalist. The naturalist seeks to tie certain moral judgements analytically to a certain *content*. This really is to try to make verbal legislation do the work of moral thought. My own theory does not get the content into our moral judgements by verbal legislation; *we* have to put it in by exploring the logical possibilities. There are real alternatives between which we have to choose. But unless we are prepared to take the fanatical line, and opt for a certain principle regardless of even our own desires, we have to allow our choices to be circumscribed by the desires of other people. This is the logical consequence of universalizability, when coupled with prescriptivity.

What circumscribes the moral prescriptions that the non-fanatic can accept is, on my theory, not (as is the case with naturalism) a verbal restriction on the content of moral judgements; it is rather the desires and inclinations of the human race. On my view, there is absolutely no content for a moral prescription that is ruled out by logic or by the definition of terms. Another feature of my position, allied to this one, is that there is no statement of fact that a moral prescription, taken singly, can be inconsistent with. On the other hand, a moral prescription can be inconsistent with other moral prescriptions, or with prescriptions of other kinds. It is this logical impossibility of combining certain prescriptions with each other that restricts the moral prescriptions that we can accept, and not the impossibility of combining them with certain statements of fact. Facts come into moral arguments in a different way (6.3, 6.8, 11.2,6).

10.5. Let me illustrate these principles by considering again the 'trumpeter' example. He cannot prescribe to himself, in a universalizable way, to play the trumpet in the given circumstances, because this would involve prescribing universally that all people in precisely his circumstances should play the trumpet. The same is true if for 'prescribe' we read 'permit'. For he cannot issue this latter prescription (or permission) without prescribing or permitting that somebody else should do the same in the same situation even if he (the present trumpeter) were in the position of his present neighbour, and with the same desires as his neighbour now has. The matter will, I hope, become clearer if we consider *why* he will be unwilling to prescribe or permit this. There is no logical impossibility that prevents him; for it is not logically absurd to say 'Do (or, you may do) the same to me if I am ever in your situation (including having your desires)'. But, if the trumpeter is really prescribing or permitting for the hypothetical situation as if it were actual, he will not say this, unless he is a fanatic. For to say it is to prescribe or permit the frustration of his own desires. Now to prescribe the frustration of desires that I *would* have in a hypothetical situation is not self-contradictory. If it be allowed that there is an analogy between having a desire and assenting sincerely to an imperative, the point can perhaps be put formally as follows: to say '*If* I in another situation assent to the imperative "p", then, even so, not-p' is not self-contradictory; what would be self-contradictory is to say 'p, but even so not-p'. What saves the first imperative from being self-contradictory is the fact that in it the first 'p' is in quotation marks—it is not actually being issued.

If it is not self-contradictory, why should he not say it? As we have seen, a fanatic can and will say it; but why should not a non-fanatical ordinary person say it—or rather, since to say it is *eo ipso* to be a fanatic, as I have been using that term, why do not ordinary people become fanatics? The answer seems to be that, if we enter imaginatively into a hypothetical situation, and think about it *as if* it were going really to happen to us, we logically cannot have desires about it which are different from those which we would have if it *were* going to be real. This is because, whenever we desire anything, we desire it because of something about it; and, since being hypothetical and being actual are not, in the required sense, 'things about' objects or events (a hypothetical toothache, exactly like this actual one, *would* hurt as much as this actual one *does* hurt), it is impossible for there to be anything about the hypothetical similar situation which makes us desire something different concerning it. A hypothetical similar situation *is* similar.

We may say, therefore, that it is no more difficult to explain why people do not desire the frustration of the desires which they would have in hypothetical situations, than it is to explain why they do not desire the frustration of those which they are going to have in situations which they think are actually going to occur. The only real fanatics, therefore, are those who can survive the test (of which I have given examples and shall give others) of coming to believe that they themselves are really going to suffer evils like those which, for their present ends, they are proposing to inflict on others. This means that they must want the ends very much. They must, e.g., want to get rid of Jews more than they want themselves to live; or they must want to lock up homosexuals more than they want to be at liberty themselves. And it hardly needs explaining why such people are rare. How many Nazis were prepared themselves to die in concentration camps, if, by some miracle, this resulted in the Jews vanishing into thin air?

And so the trumpeter has, according to the logic of universalizability, three choices open to him. He can either stop using universalizable moral concepts, and content himself with issuing singular prescriptions (6.5, 9.2). Or he can be a fanatic to the extent of prescribing that the desires which he would have in hypothetical situations should be disregarded if they conflict with the fulfilment of the ideal which he now has (9.4 ff.). Or he can, as most of us should, recognize that he cannot (given the requirement of universalizability) prescribe, or even permit, the disregarding of his neighbour's desires. It is by facing us with this threefold choice that the logic of the moral concepts, as we have interpreted them, brings most of us to accept moral principles which enable us to live with one another.

10.6. The contrast between my own theory and naturalism can be brought out in another way. According to naturalism, there are certain moral judgements which, although they are thought by most people to be judgements of substance, can be established by appeal to the uses of words. This is not so on my theory. To be more exact, in both cases there is something else that is appealed to. In the case of naturalism it is non-moral facts. For example, some variety of naturalism might say that, given certain non-moral facts about an action, we cannot, logically, deny that it was courageous—a moral judgement. Now there are no non-moral facts, on my theory, which can have this effect. My theory, indeed, allows for our normal use of non-moral facts as part of the ingredients of a moral argument (6.3); but, unlike naturalism, it says that they cannot be the sole ingredient besides logic. If a man is to be compelled to a moral conclusion, he must assent to, or be unable to assent to, certain singular prescriptions (and this will depend on what desires he has), and must treat the desires of others as if they were his own. The essential other ingredient is (to use an old-fashioned term) something *volitional*.

It must be emphasized again that the 'trumpeter' argument is not a *deduction from the fact that* the trumpeter or his neighbour has certain desires or assents to certain singular prescriptions or their contradictories. If this were my view, I should be espousing a form of naturalism akin to that form often called 'old-fashioned subjectivism'—i.e. the view that there can be deductions of moral judgements from statements about people's attitudes, &c. This kind of view is open to all the objections against naturalism, as well as to others of its own.[1] My own view is rather that, if a man is thinking morally (or even, in general, evaluatively) he is compelled to universalize his volitions; his judgements remain prescriptive, and therefore cannot be deduced from any statements of fact. And there are only two ways of universalizing one's volitions: that which makes them universal regardless of the volitions of other people (and the only person who can do this is the fanatic, who is prepared to pursue an ideal to the frustration of all his own desires, actual, or hypothetical and treated as actual); and that which tailors the universal form of them to fit the particular volitions which other people have, and which, therefore, are treated as if they were one's own.

The moral philosopher has no reason to be disturbed by the logical possibility of people becoming fanatics without self-contradiction. If someone comes to him and says 'I am going to pursue such and such an ideal regardless of everybody's interest; convince me by argument that I ought not to' the right answer is that adumbrated in *LM* 4.4: 'Let him try'. But the full force of this reply is not brought to bear unless it is realized that the fanatic has to be prepared that his prescription should be carried out as much when he is at the receiving end as when he is in his present position. Let us suppose that we are omnipotent, and can say to the would-be fanatic: 'We have arranged for there to be a special planet for people like you, in which you would be allowed to pursue your ideal, on condition that you played, in strict rotation, the roles of yourself and of all those affected by your policy, one

---

[1] See my article 'Ethics' in *Concise Encyclopedia of Western Philosophy and Philosophers*, ed. J. O. Urmson.

by one'. It is only if he can accept such a prospect that the fanatic is sincere in his fanaticism.

10.7. So then, what of the man who says 'You are a liberal, and your concepts, which you want me to use, are tainted with your liberalism. I wish to use other concepts, and I am not going to be constrained not to, any more than you are going to be constrained to use those offered you by naturalists. You must play the game and universalize your own philosophical prescriptions; you forbid the naturalist the easy move of saying "These are the moral concepts, and if you use them you will have to say so and so"; and so you cannot allow yourself the easy move (essentially the same move) of saying to me "These are the moral concepts, and if you use them your only alternatives are to be a fanatic or a liberal". I am not going to be either a fanatic or a liberal; I am simply going to stop using your concepts'? The answer to this attack should now be apparent. We could take the line which we took with the naturalists because the concepts which they employ are good fat substantial concepts, incapsulating determinate moral principles. For example, the concept 'courageous' incapsulates a certain view about what one ought to do in situations of danger. If I may be permitted to put it so, the concepts of the naturalist are not formal. And this has the consequence that we can say to the naturalist that we wish to adopt concepts different from his in their content, but having the same universally prescriptive form, and to insist on remaining free to do this.

But the concepts on which *we* rely are too meagre and formal to have this done to them. Indeed, they are so meagre (being defined merely in terms of universality and prescriptivity) that when I first sketched them out in *The Language of Morals* it was thought that no theory of moral argument could be founded on them alone, and that therefore I must be an irrationalist. But what was thought to be their weakness turns out to be their strength. It is possible to escape from naturalistic concepts and from the universal prescriptions which they incapsulate by fleeing to *other* universal prescriptions and hence to *other* concepts of the *same* form. But if a man wants to escape from my concepts, where is he going to flee to? To singular prescriptions, expressing selfish desires? Or to universal but non-prescriptive judgements? He is at liberty to take either of these courses; but if he does so, he will not disturb us. For then, though we shall still be in dispute with him about *what to do*, or about *what the facts are*, we shall no longer be in dispute with him about *what we ought to do*. We are in a position to say to him, 'If you do not consent to talk in our terms, the remaining points of dispute between us will be such as can be expressed without using any terms that anybody could call moral or even evaluative. We are ready to have disputes with you of all kinds, but let us keep the kinds distinct.' But a naturalist cannot say this to us. For if we think that what is commonly called 'courage' is not a good thing, and therefore abandon this concept as incapsulating an attitude which we have rejected, we are still left having with the people who still use the concept a very substantial dispute, which has to be expressed in terms of evaluative moral words like 'ought'.

It is not, I repeat, a question of what sounds are used in various languages to mean various things (any more than is the case in mathematics). It is rather that there is this concept 'ought', which we have all learnt the use of (though perhaps less-developed cultures have not); and, having it, we are able to distinguish it from other concepts (as, also, we can distinguish the concept of adding from that of subtraction), and thus to tell when we are having a dispute about what one ought to do, and when we are having some other kind of dispute. We are therefore able to point out to the naturalist that, though he is entitled to use his concepts, the mere existence of ours opens up a field of dispute more general than they can express, and one with which the moral philosopher is called upon to deal, but which is outside the scope of a naturalist moral philosophy. If, on the other hand, our present attacker tries to say the same thing to us, we can reply that we agree with him that there are disputes which are properly expressed in terms of his non-prescriptive or non-universalizable concepts—only our own moral philosophy is sufficiently general to allow for them.

The word 'general' is the key to the whole problem. We can get the better of the naturalist because there are crucial moral problems with which his account of the matter is not sufficiently general to deal; we can get the better of our present attacker because our language is general enough to express any dispute which he may say he is having with us. If A has a language in which he can express everything that B wants to say, and more, then A is bound to be the winner in this philosophical game. A mathematician who knows about fractions *and* integers is in a strong position *vis-à-vis* one who knows only about integers. And I claim that we are in the same position with regard both to the naturalists and to our present attacker. For our language admits of descriptive terms (as required by the naturalist); but it includes also evaluative terms, in our sense (i.e. universally prescriptive terms), which he cannot admit, but which are required in order to express things that we say.[1] And our language contains means of expressing all that our present attacker could wish to say, but also means of expressing universal prescriptions, such as his language forbids him to utter. And so, when both these factions have had their say, we shall be left saying something else which they cannot express, but which we all know perfectly well how to express—namely moral and other evaluative judgements.

---

[1] The naturalist might say that in his language what we call evaluative judgements could be expressed by means of universal imperatives. But they cannot, because the imperatives of ordinary language cannot be properly universal (*LM* 12.4). The old non-naturalists were, in this sense, right to claim that moral concepts are *sui generis*.

11 · A PRACTICAL EXAMPLE

11.1 WHAT is needed, in order to consolidate the theoretical suggestions which I have put forward, is to apply them to an important moral problem such as confronts us in real life. This will serve both to illustrate and to recapitulate the chief theses that I have been defending. The best problem, for this purpose, that I can think of is that which arises when there is conflict between races—especially between races of different colours. Allusion has already been made to this problem; but it deserves a more extended treatment. By 'more extended', I do not mean a comprehensive treatment; for that would take us out of philosophy altogether into history, sociology, psychology, and politics. Any treatment which does not include contributions from these other fields is bound to be truncated and superficial; for we need to know why (historically and psychologically) people give way to racial bitterness, and what changes in social conditions would remove it. In discussions of this problem, we very soon discover that there are many people who are quite unable to adopt the philosophical approach to it which looks for rational arguments and is prepared to test their cogency. It is no use hoping by philosophy alone to convince such people or to make them change their behaviour. Here a deep understanding of psychology is required before any progress can be hoped for. Moreover, it would be necessary in any adequate treatment of the problem to consider the scientific basis, if there is one, of the classification of people into races, and of the grading of these races in respect of intelligence and other qualities (if such grading is possible, which seems doubtful). But nevertheless there *is* a philosophical problem involved, whose neglect will also make any account of the matter superficial.

We need not only to know the causes of behaviour, and how it might be altered, but to determine what is right and wrong about the way people behave; and to this end we must examine, as I have tried to do in this book, how it is possible to reason cogently about moral questions. Therefore I make no apology for devoting this chapter to the philosophical aspects of the problem alone.

I will start with a brief and general classification, with examples, of arguments that might be used by people when faced with conflicts between races. I do not hope to make this classification very profound or complete; for I am aiming only to produce instances of the chief sorts of argument that are of logical interest. I shall start with arguments concerned with matters of fact; and I shall subdivide these into those concerned with genuine matters of fact, and those concerned with questions which look like questions of fact but turn out not to be. I shall then consider various moral arguments which could still go on even when the facts are agreed. I hope that this classification will be of some philosophical interest, as shedding light on the relation between facts and moral judgements.

11.2. First, then, genuine questions of fact. In this class, we may mention first questions about the actual characteristics of different races. And these can be subdivided into (1) questions about their capabilities; (2) questions about their moral and other propensities; and (3) questions about what it is like to *be* a member of such and such a race in such and such a situation.

(1) *The capabilities of different races*

It is sometimes said that black people are incapable of self-government, or of leadership (political or otherwise), or of acquiring an advanced education, or even certain practical skills. Now, if these allegations were true, it would have an effect on some moral arguments; for obviously it is no use maintaining that black people *ought* to be allowed to exercise self-government, if they *cannot* do so; and it is no use saying that they ought to be made foremen, if they cannot do the job of foremen. The 'argument from incapability' is not always put in this extreme form. Sometimes it is said merely that black people, though they *can* acquire these capabilities, cannot acquire them to the same degree and are therefore bound to remain inferior to white people in these respects. It is not at all clear that the weaker form of the thesis has the consequences for moral arguments which follow from the stronger form. For example, black people might not be able to govern themselves according to the standards which are said to be observed in Westminster; but this would not be an argument against the view that they ought to be allowed to govern themselves in whatever way they can. Alternatively, it may be said that black people, though they may become capable of governing themselves, &c., at some date in the distant future, are not capable of doing so now. This, if admitted, would have an important bearing on some moral questions, but not the same bearing as either of the other two theses mentioned.

(2) *The moral and other propensities of races*

It is sometimes said that members of a certain race inherit, either genetically or culturally, defects of character which might make it right to treat them differently from other races. The Jews have often been a target for such accusations; and it has also been alleged from time to time that Orientals of certain races are less truthful or less trustworthy than Englishmen claim to be. If these arrogant-sounding accusations were established, they would have some bearing on moral arguments; but how powerful it was would depend on the particular defect that existed. One would also, if the defect was inherited culturally and not genetically, have to consider to what extent the cultural and social factors causing the perpetuation of the defect were the fault of the members of the race itself, and to what extent they were the result of the actions of other races—e.g., the persecution of the Jews.

These two kinds of factual arguments are not such as can be established or refuted by philosophical reasoning. They have to be shown to be true or false by the means appropriate to the examination of alleged facts of these kinds—i.e. by the objective study of history and, in appropriate cases, by social or psychological surveys and experiments. The sincerity of people who make these kinds of allegation can, indeed, be put to the proof by seeing whether they are willing to submit to these objective tests.

(3) *What it is like to be a member of a certain race*

Another type of factual argument which may be adduced in moral disputes about race relations is concerned with the effect of certain sorts of treatment upon the happiness, &c., of the members of a certain race. Thus, it has sometimes been maintained that to use black people as slaves, or in conditions resembling slavery, is not cruel in the same way as it would be to use white people as slaves, because black people do not have the same sensibilities as white. An extreme form of this argument is the doctrine that blacks are like animals, or (it has sometimes even been said) actually *are* animals—though this is really a spurious factual argument and belongs in the next section. It is certainly true that if working on a farm in conditions similar to those of an ox on the same farm were no more a cause of unhappiness to a Bantu than to an ox, certain moral arguments against treating the Bantu in this way would not be available.

Now there are difficulties in assessing this kind of factual argument which there are not in the cases of the first two kinds mentioned. For there are notorious philosophical obstacles to verifying propositions about the feelings of other people. We can, however, sidestep these difficulties by saying that the difficulty of knowing what it feels like to be a Bantu is, at any rate, nothing like so great as that of knowing what it feels like to be an ox; and that the difficulty is one of the same kind as, and greater only in degree than, that of knowing what it is like to be James, my twin brother. The practical, as opposed to the philosophical, difficulty of knowing what it feels like to be a Bantu on a farm is to be got over by a closer and more sympathetic acquaintance with individual Bantus on farms. I shall not resume until later the question of why it is relevant to moral arguments to know what it feels like to be a Bantu (11.9, 6.4 ff.).

One other more particular type of factual argument needs to be mentioned; it is not co-ordinate with the first three, but is a way of applying one or more of them to actual situations. It is sometimes said that if certain racial policies are pursued, the results will be so and so—with the implication that these results ought to be avoided at all costs, and that therefore the policy ought to be rejected. For example, it may be argued that if the pass laws are repealed, there will be no check on subversive activities by members of the subject race, and that all sorts of violence will then break out, leading eventually to a breakdown of ordered government. Or it may be argued that if the colour bar is at all relaxed, miscegenation will result (it being taken for granted that this would be an unspeakable evil). These arguments are simply examples of a type of argument which is exceedingly common in morals, and might, indeed, be said to be a constituent in any moral argument. It is of the form 'If you do *this* in *these* circumstances, what you will be doing is to bring about *these* consequences'. The effect of such an argument is to show what, *in concreto*, the person will be doing if he does what he is proposing (*LM* 4.1). In racial contexts such arguments often depend on arguments of the types already considered: e.g., it has sometimes been said that if Jews are allowed to do business without restriction, they will, because of their moral and other propensities, soon get a stranglehold on the economy of some country and use it against the interests of non-Jews; and it was sometimes said that if Indians were allowed a greater share in the government of India, there would be, because of their incompetence and corruptibility, a break-down of the high standards of administration maintained by the (British-staffed) Indian Civil Service. If such hypothetical predictions had been correct, then the further question would have arisen of whether the states of affairs predicted were worse than the states of affairs which would come into being if alternative policies were pursued. But, subject to this proviso, this is a perfectly legitimate argument in morals, if the premisses are true. That is to say, it is quite in order to try to show that the facts are such that if a certain policy is pursued then a certain moral principle will be observed or infringed; and the argument then shifts to questions of moral principle.

11.3. Let us now turn from genuine factual arguments to spurious ones. These are forthcoming from both parties to most racial questions; they are not the monopoly of those of whose policies liberals disapprove. However, I shall start with arguments which are put forward by people of whose policies the majority of my readers will disapprove; I shall thus, perhaps, the more easily display the fallaciousness of the arguments; and then I shall turn to some similar arguments, just as lacking in cogency, which are used by those who are on the angels' side.

Suppose that a Nazi argues that he has a right to persecute members of non-Germanic races because there is something in the hereditary make-up (in the 'blood', he might say) of the Germanic races which gives them a natural superiority over other races and a right to make them their subjects. This looks at first sight very like some perfectly good factual arguments that we mentioned earlier; we have the statement that the facts are such that a certain moral principle applies. But the argument suffers from two fatal weaknesses. In the first place, no determinate criterion is given for discovering whether this factor is present in the heredity or blood of any particular person. No empirical tests are offered for determining the truth of the assertion that members of Germanic races actually have this mark of natural superiority to members of other races. So the argument rests on statements of 'fact' whose truth is in principle not ascertainable; and therefore we can never know whether the premisses of the argument, or its conclusion, are true. We do not need to be logical positivists to reject this sort of argument; but if anyone does accept some kind of verification theory of meaning, he will go further, and say that the premisses of such arguments are not merely untestable but meaningless. Into this question I shall not go, merely remarking that here is an instance where a seemingly quite abstract philosophical controversy has a direct application to practical questions.

In the second place, even if the premisses of these arguments were all right, the users of them have not told us *why* the moral conclusions follow from the premisses. In order that the presence of this blood-factor in Germans should justify their domination of other races, it has to be the case that the factor confers a right to dominate; and it is hard to see why this should be so. Even if it could be proved by experiment that whenever the blood of a German has a certain chemical added to it it turns purple, and that this is so with the blood of no other race, it is not thereby established that any moral consequences follow from this. We shall have to postpone further consideration of this question until we have come back to the general question of the place of factual premisses in moral arguments.

As further examples of this type of spurious factual argument, we may mention the argument that Christians may persecute Jews, because certain Jews said on a famous occasion 'His blood be upon us and upon our children';[1] and the argument that white people may make black people their subjects, because black people are the descendants of Ham, and it says in the Bible that Noah cursed the descendants of Ham because Ham had looked at Noah's naked body when

[1] Matthew xxvii. 25.

Noah was in a drunken stupor.[1] In both cases there is no conceivable way of discovering whether an individual Jew or Bantu who is being maltreated is really the descendant of Ham, or of a member of the crowd outside Pilate's palace; and, even if they were, it is not in the least clear why this should justify their maltreatment.

11.4. Let us now consider some examples of arguments suffering from these same two defects which are often used by more respectable people. It is often said that white people ought to treat black people better because they are their brothers; or because they are, like whites, children of God. As before, no criterion is stated for determining whether an individual member of some other race is or is not my 'brother', in the extended sense, or whether he is or is not a child of God; if two people were arguing about whether the natives of a certain territory were or were not children of God, it is entirely unclear by what tests they could ever settle their argument. We cannot, indeed, deny the value of these forms of expression as metaphors; but what we need to do is to find out what they are metaphors for, and whether propositions expressed in terms of them are, when put unmetaphorically, true.

Secondly, even if it could be established beyond doubt that a certain man was my 'brother', or that he was a 'child of God', it is not clear why it follows that I ought to treat him in a certain way. What moral principles are the basis of my duties even to my real brothers, or to the children of my human father? Admittedly, if we agree, as most of us do, that we have certain duties to our real brothers, then these duties must have as their ground *something* about the relation 'being a brother of'. It would need to be elucidated what this something is—for until this is done we shall not know what is the principle involved. Has it, for example, something to do with common nurture, and does it therefore extend to foster-

[1] Genesis ix. 25.

brothers? Or has it something to do with common parenthood, and if so do both parents have to be the same or only one? If we could answer these questions, we should then know the precise features of brothers which we think to be the grounds of our duties towards them. It would then become a question whether black people, who are our brothers only in an extended sense, possess, in common with our real brothers, those features which are the grounds of our duties to our real brothers. And it is, to say the least, rather unlikely that this would prove to be the case.

The relevance to this argument of the theses of this book is the following. I have maintained (2.2 ff.) that all moral judgements are made on the basis of *something about* the thing judged (which is another way of stating the thesis of universalizability). Now it is possible that this 'something', in the present case, might be the mere biological relation, *being a brother of*. But this seems unlikely. We are therefore led to inquire what, in particular, it is about this relation that makes us accept the moral prescription that we ought to behave in certain ways to our brothers.

There are the same sort of difficulties with the expression 'child of God'. It is not obvious *a priori* that we ought to treat fellow children of God in certain ways. We require, presumably, the general premiss that God's will ought to be done, and the particular premiss that God wills his children to treat one another in certain ways. Well-known philosophical problems arise concerning both these premisses; but there is no room to discuss them here.[1]

11.5. We may notice, lastly in this class of arguments, one which can be shown to possess the same defects as these ones, but which nevertheless enjoys a certain philosophical respectability, and which is therefore worth examining in more detail. This is the argument that we ought to treat blacks in

[1] For a brief discussion, see my article in *The Listener*, 13 October 1955, p. 593.

certain ways because they are *people*. Now it must be said at
the start that this argument is in fact an attempted short cut;
it is perfectly possible, given that blacks are people, and given
also certain other assumptions, to reason cogently that they
ought to be treated in the same way as other people. This I
shall later attempt to show (11.9). But the argument is nevertheless worthless as it stands, since it suffers from the same
defects as I have already exposed. In order to turn it into
a cogent piece of reasoning, we have to bring out into the
open certain concealed steps in the argument and certain
suppressed assumptions; and the complaint to be made
against those who use this kind of argument is not that they
arrive at wrong conclusions, but that they bury the really
important and interesting factors in the arguments, and thus
conceal from us some very fundamental features of moral
arguments and of moral discourse in general. It is only by
understanding these fundamental features that the arguments
can be seen to be cogent. The short cut proposed has thus to
be condemned for two reasons: it gets to a desirable conclusion by a fallacious mode of reasoning which could also
be used to justify the most damnable conclusions; and, by
seeming to offer an easy way to this desirable conclusion,
it encourages us to leave off our study of moral philosophy
when it has reached only a very superficial level. As it stands,
the inference from 'X is a person' to 'I ought to be kind to X'
is logically no better than that from 'X is a non-Aryan' to 'I
ought to put X in the gas-chamber'.

In order to understand this, let us first notice that the
'people' argument suffers from the same defects as the
'brothers' and 'children of God' arguments. No criterion is
offered for determining whether something is a person or not.
Is it sufficient to be a live member of the human species? It
does not seem to follow from the fact that a black person is
a live member of the human species that I ought to treat him
in any particular way. So if we have *this* determinate criterion

for being called a person, no moral conclusion seems to follow from the fact that someone is a person. The same will be the case whatever determinate criterion we are given. For example, it may be said that someone is a person if he has the power of rational choice. But it will still not be obvious why a human being who has this power ought to be allowed to exercise this choice as much as possible; for no grounds have been given for this contention.

Suppose, in general, that there is a determinate criterion for deciding whether a given being is a person or not. It will then require establishing that we ought to treat such a being in one way rather than in another. Faced with this challenge, a defender of this type of argument might make his principle indubitable by making it analytic. He might say that by establishing that X is a person one has established that X ought to be treated as a person; and that this is analytic, because 'as a person' means merely 'as a person ought to be treated'. But though it is, certainly, analytic that people ought to be treated as people ought to be treated, the question is, How ought people to be treated?

One way that might be suggested for getting out of this difficulty is to write into the notion of a person some moral content. By calling a being a person we should then imply, as part of what we are saying, that he ought to be treated in a certain way. This will validate the step from 'X is a person' to 'X ought to be treated in a certain way'. But now we are left without a determinate and morally neutral criterion for finding out whether he *is* a person. In order to be sure that he is a person, we shall first have to satisfy ourselves that he ought to be treated in a certain way, and no basis has yet been established for making this moral judgement.

11.6. Having dealt with a number of arguments which are unsatisfactory, and with others which are incomplete, in that they appeal to antecedent moral principles, we come now to the constructive part of this chapter. It is based on the account of moral language and moral reasoning given in the preceding chapters and in my earlier book.

Let us ask, first, why it is that we think what I have called factual arguments to be relevant to moral questions. Why did I say that certain factual arguments (for example about the predictable results of certain policies) were perfectly admissible; and why, on the other hand, do we have this strange phenomenon of Nazis and others inventing obviously spurious factual arguments in order to justify their actions morally? Why not just get on with the job of exterminating the Jews? What need is supplied by the bogus claim that Germans have some special element in their heredity·which distinguishes them from other men? Or why does it make a difference to the moral argument that a certain policy would have a certain result? It looks as if facts (or some sorts of facts) are held to be relevant to moral arguments; so much so that if one has not got any genuine facts one invents some make-believe ones. But why is this? In short, what is the bearing of facts on moral arguments? This is one of the central problems of moral philosophy, and I have tried in this and my earlier book to sketch an answer to it. Without further references back, let us set out the answer as clearly and briefly as possible.

An obvious, and so far as it goes true, but incomplete answer to the question 'Why are facts relevant to moral arguments?' is this: moral judgements have to be *about something*; and it is the facts of the case which determine what we are judging. Thus, when we are asking moral questions about a proposed action, it is relevant to know what the person would be doing who did the action; for, if we do not know this, we literally shall not know what we are talking about.

I say that this answer is incomplete for two reasons. The first is that it does not explain why we think some facts, and not others, relevant to moral arguments. The second is that it does not explain why it makes a difference if it is a *moral* argument. If I were deciding just what *to do*, without any thought of what I *ought* to do, it would still be important to me to know *what* I should be doing if I did so and so. We shall see that these two incompletenesses are related to each other.

There are some philosophers, to whom I have referred often enough before, who can see only one possible way in which facts might have relevance in moral arguments. This is by there being some logical link, holding in virtue of the meanings of words, between factual premisses and moral conclusions. Now I do not think that there is any such link. And because these philosophers have eyes only for this sort of relevance, they think that if I deny the possibility of such a link, I am committed to holding that facts are not relevant to moral arguments; and this would be an absurd position. But what I have been maintaining is that facts are relevant to moral arguments, but not in the way that these people think.

Facts are relevant to moral arguments because they make a difference between cases which would otherwise be similar. Let us illustrate this by considering again why the Nazis set so much store by the claim that there is something in the blood of Germans which differentiates them from other races. The explanation is that they were proposing to treat other races in a markedly different way from Germans, and wanted a reason why they *ought* to do this. A Nazi might say, as he contemplated the Jews that he was just driving into the gas-chamber, 'These men look just as I would look if I were starved and naked like them; they have the same feelings and aspirations, and there is, apparently, no other relevant difference between them and myself or my German friends. And I would not think it right to treat a German in this way. But there is something that makes a difference; although Germans and Jews are often indistinguishable to the naked eye, there is this all-important thing about them, that they lack that factor in their heredity which true Germans have, and which entitles Germans to send them to the gas-chamber.' Put thus crudely, the argument sounds grotesque; yet something of the sort undoubtedly lies behind many claims of racial superiority. And this parody of moral thinking, just because it is a parody of moral thinking, illustrates extremely well the role which even bogus facts can play in moral arguments—even bad ones. This argument of the Nazis is pretending to be like a perfectly good moral argument, and thus shows us something about what a good moral argument would be like.

The point is this: it is part of the meanings of the moral words that we are logically prohibited from making different moral judgements about two cases, when we cannot adduce any difference between the cases which is the ground for the difference in moral judgements. This is one way of stating the requirement of universalizability which, as we have seen, is fundamental to all moral reasoning. Since the Nazi cannot justify his different treatment of Germans and Jews without adducing some difference between their cases, he invents a difference.

Other participants in race conflicts are more fortunate: they do not have to invent anything; the difference is there, for all to see, in the colour of their victims' skins. This is why it seems so much easier to justify racial discrimination when there is a colour difference than when there is not. But even less obvious differences than those of colour will serve if they have to. What is important to the would-be discriminator is that there should be *some* qualitative difference (i.e. not merely a numerical difference) between the class of people whom he wishes to oppress, exploit, or persecute and those whom he does not. Some of us remember how, at school, the wearing of shoes of a different pattern was enough to mark out some poor boy for maltreatment.

These caricatures of moral reasoning teach us something about the real thing. It is indeed required that, to justify different treatment of people, qualitative differences have to be produced between them or between their actions or

circumstances. We try to justify our singular moral judgements by producing principles involved in them: one may or
ought to do such and such a *kind* of thing in such and such a
kind of situation to people of a certain *kind*.

11.7. Now these examples of spurious moral reasoning are
parodies. The question which next arises, therefore, is, How
do we distinguish the parody from its original? If we do not
think that it is an adequate justification for discriminating
against a person that his skin is black, how would we distinguish those features of the man or his situation which do
justify different treatment from those which do not? There
seems at first sight to be no formal difference between saying
'It is right to kill him because his skin is black' and saying
'It is right to kill him because he has killed another man'.
Some people regard both of these as good reasons; some,
neither; and some, one but not the other. We have therefore
to ask, can moral philosophy point out any means of distinguishing between good and bad reasons of this sort; or, in
other words, between relevant differences, such as really do
justify discrimination, and those which are not relevant?
Have we any reason for saying that black skin is not relevant,
but being a murderer is?

There are those who try to answer this question in the
following way. They take a look at the kind of differences that
people *do* call morally relevant; and they make a list of them,
reduce them if they can to some sort of system, and then say
that we *mean* by 'morally relevant difference' just these differences and no others, and *mean* by 'morality' just that system
of evaluations which takes these, and no other, differences
into account. There are many objections to this procedure;
I will here mention just two. First, how do we know that we
could not get a different list if we did the investigation in
South Africa or Soviet Russia or ancient Sparta? Secondly, to
make such a list does not explain anything; we want to know
what leads to things getting put on the list or left off it. The

proponents of this view do not seem to have gone far enough in their search for an explanation.

Now, if the argument of this book is correct, we can in fact go a good deal further, by a step which is really no different in principle from one which we took a moment ago. We saw that it follows from the meanings of the moral terms that if different moral judgements are made, relevant differences must be adduced; and we saw that this was a version of the requirement of universalizability. But we have not yet exhausted the potency of this principle; we still have the use of it left which was explained in 6.8 and 9.4.

In order to illustrate this use again, let us suppose that we are having an argument with a man who maintains that a black skin, by itself, is a sufficient ground for discriminating against its possessor. We tell him, and he, being a credulous person, believes, the following story. The Soviet Institute of Race Relations (which is a much more enterprising and scientific body than its Western counterparts) has just succeeded in breeding a new kind of bacillus, which Soviet agents are at this very moment broadcasting in areas of racial conflict throughout the world. This bacillus is very catching, and the symptom of the disease which it induces is that, if the patient's skin was white, it turns permanently black, and vice versa. Now when the person with whom we are arguing has absorbed the implications of this story, we ask him whether he still thinks that skin-colour by itself is a sufficient ground for moral discrimination. It is unlikely that he will go on saying that it is; for then he will have to say that if he catches the disease the former blacks who have also had it will have acquired the right to oppress *him*, and all his formerly white friends.

What do we learn from this simple piece of science fiction? What we have got our opponent to do by this innocent deception is to perform an intellectual operation which, if he had really been wanting to reason morally, he would have performed without the deception. This operation is to consider the hypothetical case in which he himself has lost the quality which he said was a sufficient ground for discrimination, and his present victims have gained it—and to consider this hypothetical case as if it were actual. There are two stages in the process of universalization. The first is passed when we have found a universal principle, not containing proper names or other singular terms, from which the moral judgement which we want to make follows, given the facts of our particular situation. This stage is comparatively easy to pass, even for the proponent of the most scandalous moral views. It is passed, for example, by adducing the principle that it is all right for black people to be oppressed by white people. But the next stage is more difficult. It is necessary, not merely that this principle should be produced, but that the person who produces it should actually hold it. It is necessary not merely to *quote* a maxim, but (in Kantian language) to *will* it to be a universal law. It is here that prescriptivity, the second main logical feature of moral judgements, makes its most decisive appearance. For willing it to be a universal law involves willing it to apply even when the roles played by the parties are reversed. And this test will be failed by all maxims or principles which look attractive to oppressors and persecutors on the first test. It will indeed be found that, if we apply these two tests, both founded on the logical, formal features of moral terms, we shall be able to sort out, in the field of race relations at least, the grounds of discrimination which we are really prepared to count as morally relevant from those which we are not.

11.8. From this satisfactory conclusion, however, there is, as we have seen, a way of escape for the sufficiently determined racialist. It remains to illustrate, in terms of the present example, what price he has to pay for his escape. Let us suppose that there is a racialist the mainspring of whose racialism is a horror of miscegenation; and let us suppose that the source of this horror is not any belief about the consequences, social or biological, of miscegenation. That is to say, he is not moved by alleged facts about the weakening of the human stock by mating between people of different colours, or about the unsatisfactory life lived by people of mixed descent, or by anything of that kind. If these were his grounds, we could argue with him in a scientific way, trying to show that the offspring of mixed marriages are just as likely to be vigorous and intelligent as those of other marriages; or that any bad social effects of miscegenation would be removed if *he* and people like him abandoned their attempts to enforce a colour bar. Let us suppose, however, that his grounds are not these, but simply a horror of the very idea of a black man mating with a white woman. This cannot be touched by any scientific or factual argument of the sort described. And it may well be true that, if miscegenation is to be prevented, it is necessary to have a rigid colour bar; and that if this is enforced, and leads to resentment, other repressive measures will be necessary for the maintenance of public order, and thus we shall have the whole apparatus of racial repression. If this is true, then it will be hard for us to argue with this man. He detests miscegenation so much that he is prepared to live in a police state in order to avoid it.

And he must be prepared for more than this. He must, if he is going to universalize his moral judgements, be prepared that he himself should not merely live in a police state, but live in it in the same conditions as he is now prepared to make the blacks live in—conditions which are getting steadily worse. He must be prepared that *he* should be subject to arbitrary arrest and maltreatment just on grounds of skin colour, and to butchery if he tries, in collaboration with his fellows, to protest.

Now it may be that there are people so fanatical as to be prepared for all these things in order to avoid miscegenation. But they are surely very few. The repression happens because these few people have on their side a multitude of other people who are not prepared at all to suffer thus, but who have not really thought through the argument. They think, perhaps, that all will be well without too much repression; or that blacks do not mind being treated like this as much as whites would; or that there is a scientific basis for belief in racial superiority—or some of the many other things that racialists tend to believe. All these beliefs can perhaps be refuted severally by scientists and others without any help from the philosopher; but they are apt, collectively, to form an amalgam in the minds of racialists which makes into allies of the fanatic many people who are not, in themselves, in the least fanatical. The contribution of the philosopher is to take this amalgam apart, deposit such beliefs as are open to scientific refutation in the in-trays of the scientists, and, when the scientists have dealt with them, exhibit the prescriptive remainder of racialism for what it is—something that fanatics may hold but which the bulk of a people—even a people as hard-pressed as the white South Africans—never will.

11.9. We are now in a position to explain why, in spite of the inadequacy of an argument which we mentioned earlier, it *is* morally relevant that blacks are people. Saying that they are people is saying that they are like us in certain respects. It is not clear yet in *what* respects; this will be found to vary from case to case, as we shall see. But the principle of this argument from the fact that blacks are people can now be exposed as follows. If a black man whom I am contemplating maltreating has, as I have every reason to suppose that he has, certain characteristics in common with myself—if, to use an example from an earlier century, it causes him great suffering if he and his wife are separated and sent as slaves to different countries—then I can reason as follows. I am not prepared in general to accept the maxim that it is all right for people to separate husbands from wives for commercial gain; for this would be committing myself to the judgement that it would be all right for somebody to do this to me if he were in a position to do so. But can I say that it is all right to do this to blacks? The answer must be 'No'; for if I envisage myself becoming a black, but retaining my other characteristics, and in particular the characteristic of being attached to my wife, I am not (since I am not a fanatic for the liberty of commerce) prepared to accept a maxim which permits people to do this to me.

On the other hand, if we take the example of the murderer mentioned above, the position is altered. I may very well be prepared to prescribe that, if I commit a murder, I should be hanged. In actual fact I am not; for I am not a supporter of capital punishment—for reasons which are irrelevant to the present argument. But let us, in order to avoid this difficulty, substitute 'put in prison' for 'hanged' or 'killed'. I am prepared to prescribe that if I commit a murder I should be put in prison: and my reasons are utilitarian ones comparable to those given by the judge in 7.2 ff. But reasons of this sort are not available to racialists. Thus we see why it is thought not to be relevant that the man is black, but is thought to be relevant that a man is a murderer. More important, we see why it is thought to be relevant that a slave loves his wife. The duties which we acknowledge towards people are not derived from the 'essence of man' or from any philosophical mystifications of that sort; they are acknowledged because we say 'There, but for my good fortune, go I. That man is like me in important respects; in particular, the same things as cause me to suffer cause him to suffer; therefore, unless I am prepared to accept a maxim which would permit me to be treated like him were I to acquire a black skin (which I am not), I cannot say that it is all right for me to treat him thus.'

This line of reasoning also helps to explain why we recognize certain duties towards both men and animals, but certain others towards men only. For example, nobody would be thought to be oppressing animals because he did not allow them self-government; but, on the other hand, it is generally thought to be wrong to torture animals for fun. Now why is it that we do not acknowledge a duty to accord animals self-government? It is simply because we think that there is a real and relevant difference between men and animals in this respect. We can say 'If I were turned into an animal, I should stop having any desire for political liberty, and therefore the lack of it would be no hardship to me'. It is possible to say this even of men in certain stages of development. Nobody thinks that children ought to have complete political liberty; and most people recognize that it would be foolish to introduce the more advanced kinds of political liberty all at once in backward countries, where people have not got to the stage of wanting it, and would not know what to do with it if they got it. So this mode of reasoning allows us to make the many distinctions that are necessary in assessing our obligations towards different *kinds* of people, and indeed of sentient beings. In all cases the principle is the same—am I prepared to accept a maxim which would allow this to be done to me, were I in the position of this man or animal, and capable of having only the experiences, desires, &c., of him or it?

It may be objected that not all people will follow this mode of reasoning which I have been suggesting. Those who indulged in bear-baiting did not reason: 'If we were bears we should suffer horribly if treated thus; therefore we cannot accept any maxim which permits bears to be treated thus; therefore we cannot say that it is all right to treat bears thus.' And no doubt there are some white South Africans (a few) who will be quite unmoved by being told that they are causing the Bantu to suffer. It seems that I am required to say what has gone wrong in such cases.

A number of different things may have gone wrong. The commonest is what we call insensitivity or lack of imagination. The bear-baiter does not really imagine what it is like to be a bear. If he did, he would think and act differently. Another way of putting this is to say that these people are not paying attention to the relevant similarities between themselves and their victims. If we like to revert to the metaphor, having understood what it stands for, the bear-baiter is not thinking of the bear as his brother—or even cousin.

It is also possible that, though fully aware of what they are doing to their victims, they are not reasoning morally about it. That is to say, they are not asking themselves whether they can universalize their prescriptions; though they may make play with the moral *words* which they have heard other people use, they are not, in their own thinking, using these words according to the logical rules which are implicit in their meaning. And there are other possibilities, too numerous to mention here, which have been examined in the body of this book.

It may be asked: What is to be done about this? Can the philosopher, in particular, do anything about it? When South African believers in white supremacy read this book, will they at once hasten to repeal the pass laws and make the blacks their political equals? This is highly unlikely; and in any case they will not read the book. To get people to think morally it is not sufficient to tell them how to do it; it is necessary also to induce in them the wish to do it. And this is not the province of the philosopher. It is more likely that enlightened politicians, journalists, radio commentators, preachers, novelists, and all those who have an influence on public opinion will gradually effect a change for the better—given that events do not overtake them. Perhaps people in areas of racial conflict can be, in the end, brought to think of the resemblances between themselves and members of other races as morally relevant, and of the differences as morally irrelevant. Perhaps, even, they may learn to cultivate their imaginations. But this much can be claimed for philosophy, that it is sometimes easier to bring something about if we understand clearly what it is we are trying to do.

INDEX